WATCH YOUR MOUTH

Discover What's Alive Inside!
The Amazing Microworld of Tongue Fuzz
and Bad Breath!

by Linda Allison, Rebecca Smith, and Judy Diamond

BitingduckPress.com

WATCH YOUR MOUTH

by Linda Allison, Rebecca Smith, and Judy Diamond
Design and Illustration by William Wells

Biomedical research is transforming our understanding of the processes that affect human health. Our bodies are home to as many microbes as human cells, and the balance of helpful to harmful microbes in our bodies can make us sick or healthy. This book explores some common microbes and the many roles they play inside our mouths.

The *Biology of Human* project focuses on helping people understand themselves by exploring scientific principles that underlie modern research in human biology. *Biology of Human* is an alliance of educators, artists, science writers, social scientists, and biomedical researchers working to increase public understanding about viruses and infectious disease. For more information about our projects visit:

http://biologyofhuman.unl.edu

Biology of **HUMAN**

SEPA SCIENCE EDUCATION
PARTNERSHIP AWARD

Supported by the National Institutes of Health

WATCH YOUR MOUTH

Published by
BITINGDUCK PRESS
978-1-938463-28-0 (print)
978-1-938463-29-7 (electronic)
For information, contact
Bitingduck Press
Altadena, California

notifications@bitingduckpress.com

We nicknamed some of the microbes in this book to make them easy to remember. *Candida albicans* is full the scientific name for a fungus that can coat your tongue. Scientists sometimes shorten this to *C. albicans*. We call it Candi. Nuc, Mity, Mutans, and Denti are nicknames for other microbes we talk about in this book.

TABLE OF CONTENTS

LIFE ON YOU

You have more microbes in your mouth than there are people on Earth. That's right, the number of bacteria in your mouth can easily exceed more than six billion. For every one of those bacteria, there may be as many as a thousand viruses. And that's not counting the fungi and other organisms that call your mouth home. Horrified?

Don't be. It's quite natural to have zillions of microbes (tiny invisible life forms) living on you and in you. Most of them do you no harm and many of them do you good. It is no wonder the inside of your mouth is home base to a myriad of happy microbes – it's deliciously dark, toasty warm, and constantly washed with a moist solution of dissolved foods. It is a heavenly habitat for an abundance of tiny life forms.

However, your mouth is not just one habitat; it's a wonderland of micro habitats. Each of these mini places offers very different conditions and attracts an amazing range of tiny creatures well suited to each space. Some microbes thrive in the dark spaces between your gums and teeth. Others are right at home in the folds of your tonsils. Some prefer to float around in the warm ocean of your saliva. Some lash themselves to the hard surfaces of your teeth, forming a gooey film that helps them and their friends stick around. Each of your teeth is a neighborhood with its own mix of species. Many of your mouth organisms are choosy: Some like the front of the tongue, while others prefer the back.

There are about a thousand different kinds of microbes that can live in the human mouth, but not every microbe colonizes every mouth. Most people have between 100 and 200 kinds of microbes that call your mouth "home." Many of these are quite common, but some are rare. Your personal mix of microbes is as unique to you as your fingerprints.

Your mouth critters compete for space and nutrients. At the same time, they work together to form a complex ecosystem that enables them to stay alive and thrive. This army of friendly microbes defends you against the unfriendly microbes that are always waiting to move in.

Your resident microbes have learned to live with you. Maybe it's time you found out how to live better with them.

Tongue bacteria magnified

Hi! I'm DENTOMAN. Let me introduce you to the amazing micro world inside your mouth.

Why is he waving a toothbrush?

Chapter 1
YOUR MOUTH
A Universe of Tiny Life Forms

From a microbe's point of view, the inside of your mouth is one turbulent place. Imagine living in a neighborhood where floods of saliva gush and flush through the streets. During all hours of the day and night, a big, muscular tongue agitates the area, constantly massaging every surface. At any moment lunch, dinner or snacks can switch the temperature of your mouth from warm to hot to icy cold. Masses of salty, acidic or basic foods wash by into the stomach. If you're a tiny microbe that happens to get caught in this mushy mix of chewing and swallowing, you are flushed down the throat into a killer bath of stomach acid.

Why would any critter live in such a hostile place? Because the mouth is also a dark, moist cave with a constant supply of food. In many ways it's a great place to live…if you're able to stick around.

STICKING AROUND BY STICKING TOGETHER

So what IS a biofilm?

It is a living colony of microlife that sticks to surfaces like teeth.

A survival strategy for many mouth microbes is to put down an anchor so they don't get washed away. Biofilm is another name for the living communities of microbes that anchor to your teeth and other surfaces.

BETTER WITH BUDDIES

Many microbes have discovered life is better with buddies. When they come together in a biofilm community, there are more surfaces to stick to. Once stuck to a surface, microbes are very difficult to evict. Group life offers protection from predators and harsh substances. While a single kind of bacteria like Mutans (bio on page 36) can survive on their own, they thrive in a biofilm empire.

Biofilm coating a tooth. (highly magnified)

THEY'RE EVERYWHERE

It's @!!#! alive!

Ick!!

EMPIRE BUILDING BACTERIA-STYLE

Don't think that biofilms happen only in your mouth. They happen everywhere. The scum on your shower curtain is a biofilm. Biofilms corrode plumbing pipes and scum up water faucets. Biofilms are the slime on the bottoms of boats. Biofilms make stones slippery at the bottom of streams. Biofilms darken desert rocks. Biofilms grow everywhere there is a surface, moisture and at least a minimal amount of nutrients. Your mouth is a perfect place for biofilms to grow.

Every drop of your saliva swarms with thousands of free-floating microbes. Many of them adapt to stationary life in a biofilm. First they must find a friendly surface to stick to. Your teeth are covered with a substance called "glycoprotein" that attracts microbes.

Glycoprotein coatings change the electrical charge on a tooth surface. Microbes are attracted to this charged surface sort of the way your hair sticks to the charged surface of a balloon with static cling. Certain microbes have receptors on their surface that allow them to hang onto glycoproteins. Different microbes have evolved various ways to stick. Not every microbe will stick to every surface.

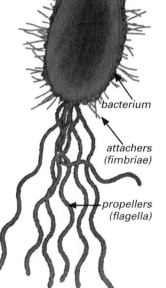

bacterium

attachers (fimbriae)

propellers (flagella)

Streptoccocus mitis

aka: Mity

DESCRIPTION

Mity is a sphere-shaped bacterium. Like its other Strep cousins, it usually grows in short chains. Some Mity strains have a furry fringe on their surfaces.

HABITAT

Many warm-blooded mammals have Mity in their mouth, nose and throat. This bacterium thrives on tooth surfaces and is one of the first microbes on the scene to anchor to a tooth and kick-start the growth of sticky biofilms. Generally, Mity lives in the mouth with no ill effects, but sometimes it can enter the bloodstream and cause infection of the heart.

LIFESTYLE

This hardy bacterium thrives in both high- and low-oxygen environments. It grows well at warm temperatures ranging from 30 to 35º C (86–95º F), so your mouth is a perfect climate.

SPECIAL TALENTS

Mity is an excellent sticker. Its ability to glom onto surfaces makes it one of the first microbes to join tooth biofilms. As other microbes crowd into the biofilm community, they use up much of the available oxygen. Mity's ability to switch to a low–oxygen lifestyle is a handy trick for coping with a changing habitat.

Saliva contains defense chemicals that discourage microbes from settling on a tooth surface. Some strains of Mity have special talents: They can produce an enzyme that can break down the saliva defense chemicals.

FAMILY NEWS

Mity and its cousin Mutans are members of the same family of bacteria, called Streptococcaceae. Mity and Mutans have a more dangerous cousin, the bacterium that causes strep throat (Streptococcus pyogenes).

Members of the strep family have been living on humans for eons. For thousands of years, humans have used the talents of this bacterial clan to make yogurt and cheese.

> **FACT:** *Bacterium is the word for a single microbe. Bacteria means more than one. In real life it is unlikely you will ever meet a single bacterium because there are such vast numbers of them everywhere.*

FROM FLOATER TO STICKER

Microbes like Mutans float around the mouth living a freewheeling life. When a Mutans bumps up against a friendly surface, it starts to settle down. Suddenly, different genes switch on inside its body and it changes personality. It transforms from a floater to a sticker. Mutans uses structures like tentacles to anchor to the tooth. Biologists describe this shift as changing from a

 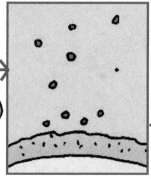

freefloating lifestyle to an anchored member of a biofilm community.

> **FACT:** *Even after a cleaning at the dentist, teeth don't stay naked for long. Within a fraction of a second, the "naked" tooth enamel acquires a thin coating of glycoproteins from your saliva.*

BIOFILM PIONEERS

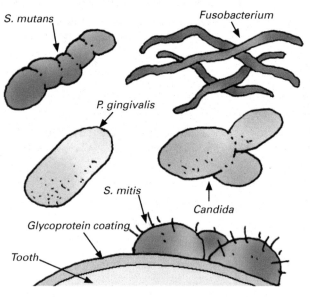

S. mutans

Fusobacterium

P. gingivalis

S. mitis

Candida

Glycoprotein coating

Tooth

Certain microbe species are especially good at forming the first anchors, making them pioneers on a tooth surface. Later, other microbes floating around the mouth sense these anchored bacteria and lash onto them with their own sticky surfaces. Once attached, the microbe secretes a gooey matrix material. The goo acts like mortar, cementing a new microbe into the biofilm.

BUILDING THE BIOFILM

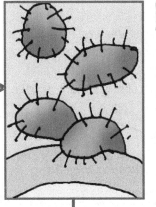

Biofilms are complex communities where bacteria form stacks, layers and channels. As more microbes join the biofilm community, different neighborhoods develop, each with its own unique environment with different levels of acids and bases, oxygen and nutrients. Sometimes one microbe's waste products become food for another microbe.

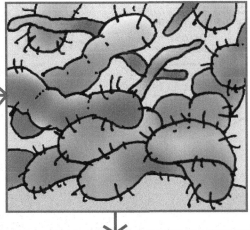

The biofilm on your teeth can harbor hundreds of different species.

BIOFILM: THE MOVIE

Picture the surface of a tooth like the wide open country of the Western frontier. At first there are a few tiny camps of hardy adventurers. Then a few more pioneer types show up. They settle down, reproduce, and soon there is a village. As different families of bacteria arrive, the little village grows into a town. The town soon expands into a city with different neighborhoods where different kinds of bacteria have specialized jobs. Before long, the city supports a dense, diverse population with new types of organisms such as fungi and other small creatures. Eventually, the region is covered with a film of settlement seething with live bodies.

Tooth bacteria highly magnified

Activity: Investigating Plaque

Yes, the goo that gives your teeth that fuzzy feel, and a yellowish tint is actually a coating of living slime. Here's how to get up close and personal with your homegrown biofilm. Do this before you brush or floss.

YOU WILL NEED:
- a mirror (a magnifying mirror is even better)
- a good source of light
- a toothpick

1. Smile. Take a good, close look at your teeth. Check out the in-between spaces and where your teeth meet the gums. Notice anything?

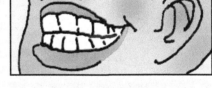

2. Gently poke a toothpick between your teeth, and under the gums. You will probably find chunks of yellowish goo. This is either plaque or the food bits packed between your teeth that provide snacks for your plaque-making bacteria.

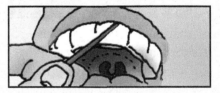

3. Rub some of the goo between your fingers. Is it smooth or sticky? Smear the gooey deposits on a sheet of dark paper. What does it look like?

4. Sniff it. Does it have a scent?

sniff

SCUM TELLS THE TALE

You say, "No way that there's bacteria growing in my mouth! I brush. I swish. I don't eat that many sweets. My mouth isn't acting like a hot, humid petri dish...teeming with microbes that eat, reproduce, spew acid and die." Think not? Just run your tongue across your teeth. Does it feel like your teeth are wearing sweaters? Notice a scummy feel? That's plaque, proof positive that bacteria are thriving on your teeth.

ABOUT THAT SMELL

That sour smell from the plaque comes from your mouth microbes at work. The plaque scrapings are a mix of bacteria, dead cheek cells, saliva and food bits. Your mouth microbes go to work feeding on the food debris in your mouth. As they digest bits of food left in your mouth, they release sulfur compounds that have a sour, stinky smell.

> **FACT:** The name for the coating of living slime on your teeth is plaque.

BACTERIA TALK

When colonies of bacteria begin to form, something surprising happens: bacteria start talking to each other. But how can a microscopic critter with no eyes, ears or sense of touch even find other bacteria in the soup of your mouth's interior, much less talk?

Bacteria communicate by sending and receiving messages made of chemical signals. This and other forms of chemical chatter let bacteria sense the presence of others. Communication between biofilm bacteria allows the entire microbial community to react or behave like a multicellular organism. Irritate one area of a biofilm, and the whole microbial community reacts.

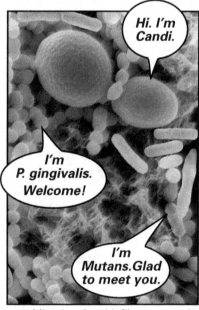

Microbes in a biofilm community

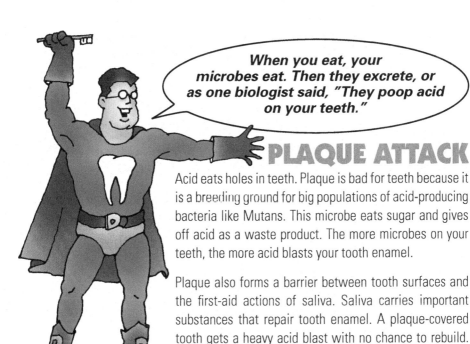

> *When you eat, your microbes eat. Then they excrete, or as one biologist said, "They poop acid on your teeth."*

PLAQUE ATTACK

Acid eats holes in teeth. Plaque is bad for teeth because it is a breeding ground for big populations of acid-producing bacteria like Mutans. This microbe eats sugar and gives off acid as a waste product. The more microbes on your teeth, the more acid blasts your tooth enamel.

Plaque also forms a barrier between tooth surfaces and the first-aid actions of saliva. Saliva carries important substances that repair tooth enamel. A plaque-covered tooth gets a heavy acid blast with no chance to rebuild. The result is that your tooth enamel develops tiny micro holes that can grow into ever-bigger holes called cavities.

LIFE OF A CAVITY

As acid continues to eat away in the tiny holes on a tooth surface, the holes grow larger. These larger holes become homes to new layers of acid-making microbes. Eventually, the microbes gradually dissolve their way through the outer enamel layer and into the softer tooth core.

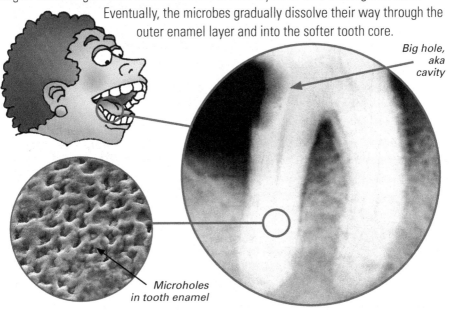

Big hole, aka cavity

Microholes in tooth enamel

Chapter 2

TOOTH ARCHITECTURE
The Inside Story

A tooth is clad in a rock-hard outer casing of enamel. Tooth enamel is amazing stuff. It is the hardest substance in the body. It is tougher than bones and even a bit harder than steel. The inside of the tooth is made of softer, more sensitive material.

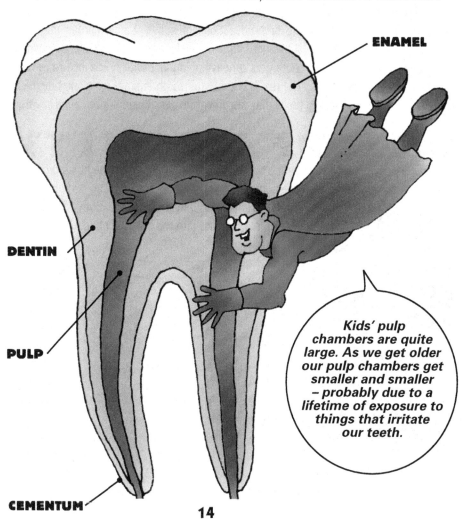

ENAMEL

DENTIN

PULP

CEMENTUM

Kids' pulp chambers are quite large. As we get older our pulp chambers get smaller and smaller – probably due to a lifetime of exposure to things that irritate our teeth.

ENAMEL

The enamel coating on your teeth is made of long mineral crystals. The crystals grow in layers between strands of protein material; 98% of tooth enamel is crystals, and the other tiny bit is water and living material. The layered structure makes enamel very strong while allowing a bit of flexibility. Because enamel is tough and shatter resistant, it's a great material to stand up to a lifetime of chewing.

PULP

The hollow interior of the tooth is called the pulp chamber. All of the living tissue in this chamber is called dental pulp. Lining the inside of the pulp chamber are cells that are able to produce new dentine. Nerves in the pulp alert the brain when something goes wrong inside the tooth. This is the most sensitive part of the tooth.

DENTIN

Under the enamel is a softer material called dentine. It is hard and thick and makes up the biggest part of the tooth. Dentin is a living tissue produced by cells that live inside the pulp chamber. Dentin is sensitive to hot and cold.

CEMENTUM

This bone-like substance covers the under-the-gums part of the tooth or root. Cementum is a mineralized tissue that helps connect a tooth to the jawbone.

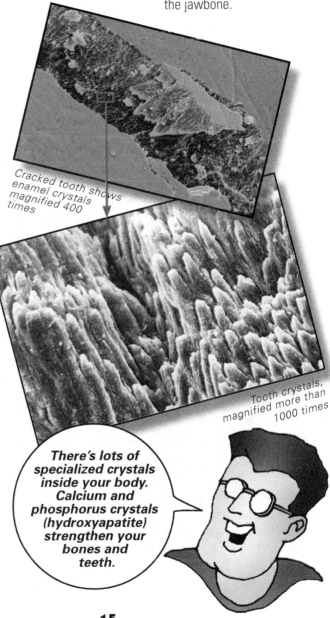

Cracked tooth enamel shows crystals magnified 400 times

Tooth crystals, magnified more than 1000 times

There's lots of specialized crystals inside your body. Calcium and phosphorus crystals (hydroxyapatite) strengthen your bones and teeth.

15

DISAPPEARING ACT

Tooth enamel may be tough as nails, but expose it to acid and the crystals in enamel will come apart. Luckily, saliva generally keeps the inside of your mouth at a tooth-friendly neutral pH. Scientists use the pH scale to measure of how acidic something is – a substance that is pH neutral is neither acid nor base. When the inside of the mouth becomes acidic, it's trouble for your teeth.

Not my problem, you're thinking? What kind of crazy person would put acid in their mouth? Ever sip lemonade? Bite into a pickle? Drink orange juice? Put ketchup on your burger? All of these foods temporarily acidify the inside of your mouth. It's easy and delicious to constantly bathe your teeth in the juice of destruction.

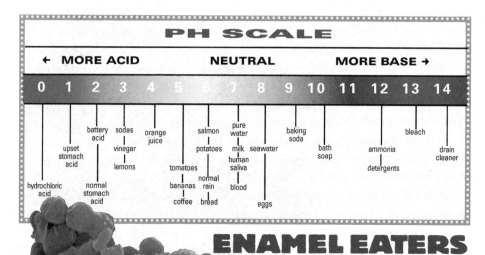

PH SCALE

← MORE ACID   NEUTRAL   MORE BASE →

| 0 | 1 | 2 | 3 | 4 | 5 | 6 | 7 | 8 | 9 | 10 | 11 | 12 | 13 | 14 |

- battery acid — sodas
- orange juice
- salmon
- pure water
- baking soda
- bleach
- upset stomach acid
- vinegar
- potatoes
- milk — seawater
- human saliva
- bath soap
- ammonia
- drain cleaner
- hydrochloric acid
- normal stomach acid
- lemons
- tomatoes
- bananas — normal rain
- blood
- detergents
- coffee — bread
- eggs

ENAMEL EATERS

Acid-producing bacteria don't lurk in your mouth waiting around to attack your teeth. Your microbes are just trying to survive while clinging to your teeth and freeloading off whatever food you happen to be eating. It is unfortunate that in the process of digesting their food Mutans and friends produce a lot of acid. Acid is tooth enamel's enemy.

S. mutans and friends

Activity: Acid Attack

Both teeth and eggshells are weakened by acid. Since most people don't have a spare baby tooth to use, you can set up an acid attack on an eggshell to see what will happen:

YOU NEED:
- an egg (or a spare baby tooth)
- a clear drinking glass
- white vinegar (any kind will work, but it is easier to see through the white kind)

1. Place the egg in the glass.

2. Cover the egg with vinegar. Watch what happens when the acid hits the shell.

3. After 24 hours gently lift out the egg. How would you describe those acid effects?

4. If you want a really strong effect, replace the vinegar with a fresh batch and check back tomorrow.

NOTICE:
Vinegar is an acid that's able to break chemical bonds. When acid sits on teeth, it breaks apart the calcium compounds that make teeth and eggshells strong. The calcium dissolves out of the eggshell or tooth into the liquid. The bubbles you see on the egg are carbon dioxide, a byproduct of the breakdown of the eggshell.

HARDCORE

Many living things use minerals to stiffen their tissues to give them strength. Seashells and bones are two examples. Even microcritters like diatoms cover themselves in mineral coats.

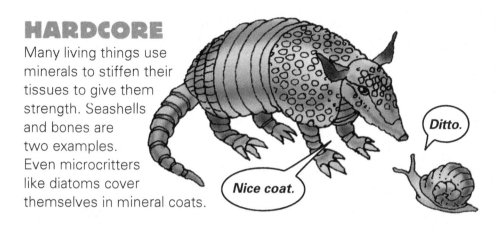

Ditto.

Nice coat.

Cracked egg shell

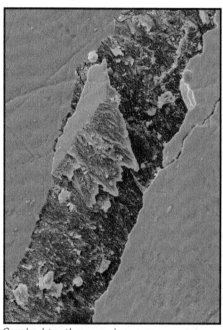

Cracked tooth enamel

BIOMINERALS

Tooth enamel and eggshells are not made of the same material, but they share some common properties. Both are biominerals. Biominerals are substances like bone that a living thing has converted to a mineral. Both teeth and eggshells use calcium to create hard coatings. Calcium phosphate makes up 99% of tooth enamel. Eggshells are mostly made of chalky calcium carbonate that is softer than calcium phosphate (a good thing in an egg, otherwise the chick might have a hard time getting out). Acid dissolves the minerals out of biominerals. Both teeth and eggshells are weakened by acid.

Activity: Fluoride Protection?

Does your dentist ever suggest a fluoride rinse to protect your teeth? Think it works? Here is how to test if a fluoride rinse will protect an egg from an acid attack.

YOU NEED:
- 2 eggs
- 2 clear drinking glasses
- fluoride rinse (ACT rinse, Listerine, Smart Rinse, or similar store brand) plus your adult's permission to use the rinse
- white vinegar
- a pencil or marker

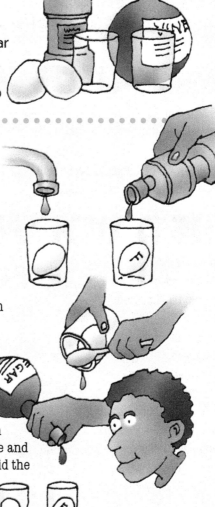

1. Mark the egg that gets fluoride. Place each egg in a separate glass.

2. Cover one egg with fluoride rinse, and the other with water.

3. Let the eggs stand overnight.

4. Next day, pour off the liquid on the eggs and cover with vinegar.

5. Watch what happens over the next couple of hours.

NOTICE: Did you see a difference in bubble action between the egg treated with a fluoride rinse and the egg put into water? How long did the fluoride effect seem to last? If bubbling is a sign the acid is breaking down the shell, what might this mean for your teeth?

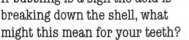

BLUE TEETH

Tooth enamel is not a uniform thickness. It is denser on the crowns where the chewing surface needs more protection, and thinner at the edges. In fact, if you shine a light into your mouth, you might see that the edges of your teeth let light through. The enamel of some people's teeth has a yellowish cast and for others a bluish cast. What color is yours? (The best place to do this is in a dark place.)

THE DAILY KNOCK DOWN

Thorough brushing and flossing removes acid-producing biofilms from your teeth. Cleaning does not eliminate biofilm-forming bacteria; it just knocks their numbers down. Even after you clean your teeth, bacteria in your mouth quickly start to form new biofilms. The daily knockdown is important. Otherwise, too many mouth bugs can overwhelm your body's defenses and tip the scale towards disease.

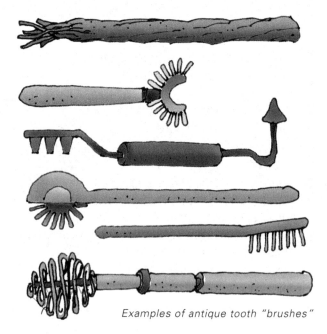

Examples of antique tooth "brushes"

They don't have to. Sharks shed teeth several times a year, and their lost teeth are replaced with new ones. This happens often, so biofilms can't build up and destroy a shark's teeth with cavities. Humans are not so lucky; we only get two sets of teeth. Most surfaces of the human body slough off cells on a regular basis, but not teeth. Our skin, hair, the linings of the mouth, nose, and intestines all shed cells continuously. In doing so, the body loses colonizing biofilms. Because teeth can't clean themselves in this way, they are targets for sticky, cavity-causing microbes. Unlike sharks, humans need to brush.

WHY SHARKS DON'T BRUSH

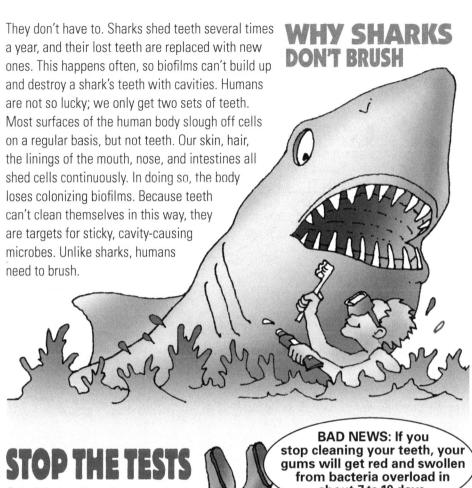

STOP THE TESTS

Swedish dental students were asked to suck sugar cubes all day long. As part of the experiment, they also agreed not to brush or floss. Researchers tracked what happened in their mouths. They found that their plaque quickly became thick and robust. When researchers peeked under the students' biofilms they found they were starting to get microcavities after one week. The researchers stopped the study so the students' teeth would not be damaged.

BAD NEWS: If you stop cleaning your teeth, your gums will get red and swollen from bacteria overload in about 7 to 10 days.

GOOD NEWS: Resume cleaning your teeth, and your gums will return to a healthy state in about a week.

LOSING IT

Once you lose it, can you get your enamel back? Yes! Microscopic cavities can be reversed thanks to the restorative powers of spit. Your saliva has concentrated amounts of calcium and phosphate. When it washes over the surfaces of your teeth, these minerals help rebuild the enamel. This slow, steady repair can fill tiny holes provided they are not too big and the biofilms have been removed.

Highly magnified tooth surface

WHAT IS FLUORIDE?

Fluoride in mineral form

Like calcium and phosphate, fluoride is a mineral. Your dentist might have told you to brush with fluoride toothpaste.

That's because applying the right amount of fluoride can kick-start, and even improve, the tooth rebuilding process. Low concentrations of fluoride often increase the growth of enamel crystals and

FACT: *About 400 million people in the world drink fluoridated water.*

make your teeth more resistant to acid attack. Toothpaste with fluoride is a really handy way to bathe your enamel with this mineral.

The very best time to fortify your teeth with fluoride is when you are a kid. A lot of cities put fluoride in the water for just this reason. When you swallow drinking water with fluoride, it gets into your bloodstream and into the developing teeth still

inside your jaw. Some of your tooth enamel's normal minerals are replaced by acid-resistant mineral fluoride.

WEIRD BROWN STAIN

Fredrick McKay, a dentist in Colorado Springs, was puzzled that so many folks in this small town had stained teeth but very few cavities. His fellow dentists called this weird condition "Colorado Brown Stain".

There were theories. Poverty caused it. Maybe it was radium in the soil or eating too much pork. Dr. McKay decided to investigate. He looked into the mouths of almost three thousand local school kids. He found 89% of them had the chocolate-colored stains. He also discovered these kids' teeth had hardly any cavities. Something was going on, but what?

Dr. McKay began his research in about 1901. It was slow going. He was a working dentist paying for most of his research himself. By 1915 he was pretty sure it was something in the water supply, but test after test turned up nothing. He began writing to others who could help with his investigation. The big breakthrough came from a chemist from Alcoa Aluminum Company who was able to run a test that detected a high amount of fluoride in the local water. By 1931 it was proved that fluoride was the cause of the stain.

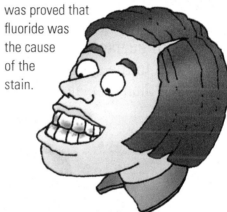

FLUORIDATION

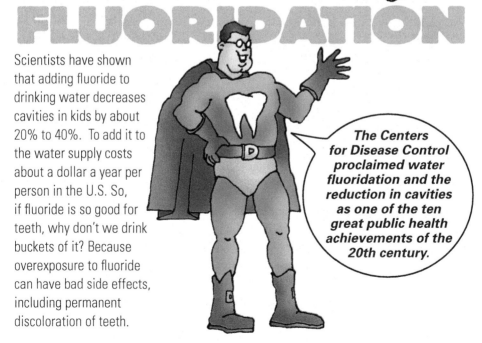

Scientists have shown that adding fluoride to drinking water decreases cavities in kids by about 20% to 40%. To add it to the water supply costs about a dollar a year per person in the U.S. So, if fluoride is so good for teeth, why don't we drink buckets of it? Because overexposure to fluoride can have bad side effects, including permanent discoloration of teeth.

The Centers for Disease Control proclaimed water fluoridation and the reduction in cavities as one of the ten great public health achievements of the 20th century.

Chapter 3

PLAQUE ATTACK

Tartar & Gum Wars

Like all life forms, microbes in plaque live and die. The dead bacteria in a biofilm harden as the minerals in saliva replace their living parts. These hardened, dead bacteria stay stuck on the tooth surfaces. More substances floating around in your saliva fill in the spaces between the hardened globs of bacteria and glue them in place.

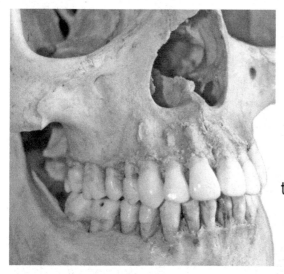

It takes about 2 days for fresh plaque to start to turn into a kind of cement that coats the tooth surface. After a few weeks it darkens and turns into a very crusty coating that can be very difficult to remove. This crusty coating is called tartar.

Tartar can stick around a LONG time

TONGUE TEST

Fresh plaque is soft and squishy and a pale white-to-yellow color. The harder yellowish grey material around your teeth near your gums is tartar. Run your tongue over the outside of your upper front teeth and you probably can detect smooth plaque-free surfaces. Do the same on the inside surfaces of your lower front teeth and it is likely that it will feel rougher. That rough feeling is mineralized deposits of plaque. As layers of tartar build up, it gets thicker and crustier.

WHAT'S THE HARM?

So why should you care if you have a little brown crust lurking where the sun don't shine? Is it a big deal? Yes! Plaque puts your teeth in danger. Plaque is a perfect nesting ground for microbes that produce gum-damaging chemicals. This is especially a problem when biofilm bacteria grow under the gums. Long-term gum inflammation from these microbes can destroy the fibers that attach the teeth to the gums and underlying bone. The result is loose teeth or worse.

Gingivitis is what dentists call early gum disease. The symptoms include bad breath, and angry, red, swollen gums that bleed when you brush or floss.

Plaque vs. tartar: What's the difference?

Plaque is fresh, squishy biofilm ... tartar is old, hard biofilm.

Soft plaque

GUM WARS

When big populations of bacteria take up residence in the shallow crevice between your gums and teeth, you get gingivitis. You know you have it when you see red, swollen gums that tend to bleed when you brush or floss. These are all signs that your body is responding to the irritating effects of the bacteria. In most cases, you can make the gingivitis go away by removing the plaque with brushing and flossing.

Hard plaque acts like splinters in the gums.

GINGIVITIS
GUMMY BATTLEGROUND

Many different microbes have adapted to living under your gums. The zone between gum and tooth is the frontier where your immune system wages a battle with these microbes. If the plaque deposits under the gums are not controlled and grow too large, the body's immune system gets an overdose of bacteria.

Your body fights back with an immune response called "inflammation." The gums become red, swollen, and sometimes tender. Sometimes you get bad breath in the bargain because the biofilm bacteria make stinky sulfur compounds (think rotten eggs) as they go about their business under the gums.

Nice smile.

> **FACT:** *Red, swollen gums from gingivitis are not rare. More than 50% of people, including kids, have them.*

INFLAMMATION: WHAT IS IT?

Inflammation is your body's response to attack or infection. When your body's surveillance system detects invaders, it turns on its defenses. Your body increases blood flow to the attack site (causing redness and heat).

Then it floods the area with liquid (causing swelling) and sends its white blood cell defenders to the area (making still more heat). If you ever had a sore throat or a splinter in your finger, you know the feelings: hot, swollen and sore.

TOOTH ATTACHMENT ANATOMY

The root of each tooth rests in a pocket in the jawbone, called a socket, while the attachments hold them firmly in place. Your tooth attachments are just as important as your teeth.

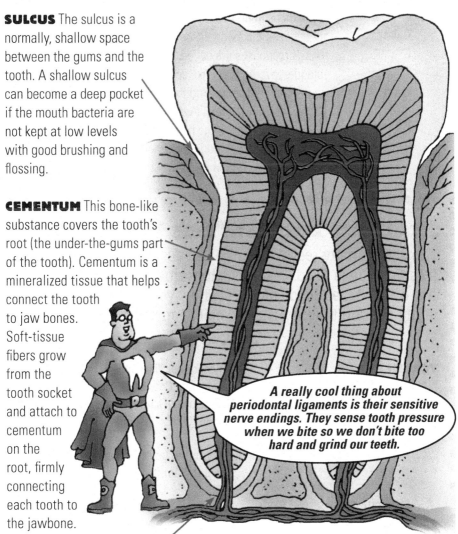

SULCUS The sulcus is a normally, shallow space between the gums and the tooth. A shallow sulcus can become a deep pocket if the mouth bacteria are not kept at low levels with good brushing and flossing.

CEMENTUM This bone-like substance covers the tooth's root (the under-the-gums part of the tooth). Cementum is a mineralized tissue that helps connect the tooth to jaw bones. Soft-tissue fibers grow from the tooth socket and attach to cementum on the root, firmly connecting each tooth to the jawbone.

A really cool thing about periodontal ligaments is their sensitive nerve endings. They sense tooth pressure when we bite so we don't bite too hard and grind our teeth.

PERIODONTAL LIGAMENT The periodontal ligament is soft tissue between the tooth and jawbone. It contains the fibers that connect the tooth to your jaw and helps cushion the teeth. It also has a large number of cells that produce bone, cementum and other important tissues.

GUMS ON THE RUN

When you get a splinter in your finger, the tissue around the microbe-infested wound gets hot, red and swollen. Pus forms. Your own flesh actually dissolves next to the microbe-covered invader, in your body's attempt to get away from the irritant. After a while the splinter gets easier to pull out because the living tissue around it shrinks away. All these body's responses are called "inflammation." Your body treats plaque-covered teeth like splinters. The body tries to remove the plaque-covered tooth with an inflammatory attack, but it doesn't work very well. Our immune system can't remove the biofilm, but it can wall it off. This is especially true in the mouth because biofilm bacteria know how to avoid the antibacterial weapons of our immune system.

Activity Part 1: Track Your Plaque

"No scum on my teeth!" Don't be so sure. A light film of fresh plaque is hard to see, but it stains beautifully. A few drops of red food color will show you where plaque is piling up. Don't worry, the red color isn't permanent.

YOU NEED:
• red food coloring
• a tablespoon
• a mirror
• a cup or glass of water
• dirty teeth (don't brush first)

1. Mix four drops of red food color with two tablespoons of water in the glass.

2. Swish the red mixture around in your mouth for 20 seconds. Then spit carefully back in the cup. Careful! Food color stains things other than plaque – like clothes and fingers!

3. Smile. Look closely in the mirror. Shocking, isn't it?

4. Hint: You can swish another 20 seconds if you want brighter stains.

NOTICE: Where are the biofilm build-ups? See any patterns?

28

WORSE GUM WARS

If the gum inflammation of gingivitis is not slowed, it can progress to a worse problem called "periodontitis." In this case the bacteria burrow deeper under the gums. Your body's own immune response damages your gums to avoid the constant irritation from the out-of-control biofilm.

Unfortunately, this gives the biofilm bacteria more room to grow and grow and grow…until the living tissue holding the tooth is destroyed. Eventually, the infection begins to attack the jawbone where the teeth are attached, making the teeth looser…if they get loose enough, they fall out.

Yikes!

Activity Part 2: Toothbrush Rescue

Did you suddenly get a strong urge to brush and floss like crazy?

1. Get out your toothbrush, dental floss and any other tools you use to clean your teeth and go to work.

2. Rinse well.

3. Now try the red color steps again.

NOTICE: Do you see any difference in the biofilm deposits after you brush?

BEFORE TOOTHPASTE

Don't hurt yourself cleaning your teeth. You can cut your gums with floss. You can puncture your cheeks and gums with a toothbrush. Tooth cleaning should be comfortable. No scrubbing!

If it hurts, you're brushing too hard.

Humans have been trying to get the scum off their teeth for thousands of years. Over time, people have invented many clever ways of cleaning teeth. The Romans cleaned with mixtures of crushed bones and oyster shells. American colonists brushed with burnt bread and tree resin. Poor folk in England resorted to rubbing their teeth with a sooty rag. Brick dust, salt, chalk, charcoal chips have all been used in powders sold to clean teeth. Developed countries use toothpaste, but some people still brush with simpler substances, like baking soda or salt.

TOOTH STICKS

Before the toothbrush, there was the stick. For thousands of years in many parts of the world, people have "brushed" with sticks. About 80% of people living in rural India start their day by chewing the end of a neem stick. Then they rub their teeth with the fringed end. The neem tree, native to South Asia, has long been prized for its healing properties. Twigs from bay, juniper, lemon, orange and eucalyptus trees have all been used as tooth cleaning sticks. Miswak sticks from the arak tree are preferred in many countries. In Africa this plant is called the "toothbrush tree."

Activity: The Brush Off

The toothbrush is a tool for knocking down biofilm. The job of toothpaste is to make your brush more effective. Try experimenting with the scum-removing power of different tooth cleaners.

YOU NEED:
- a hardboiled egg
- a glass of stain (cranberry juice, strong dark coffee or tea)
- tooth cleaners to test: favorite toothpaste, baking soda, salt
- a toothbrush
- paper towels
- a pencil
- a magnifying glass (optional)
- a timer

1. Drop an egg into the stain.

2. Remove the egg after it soaks up a good tint (5–10 minutes). Let it dry on a paper towel.

3. With a pencil, mark off 3 zones on one side of the egg.

4. Brush test: Brush one zone on the egg for one minute with toothpaste. Label the section TP for toothpaste.

5. Rinse the brush well. Brush test a different zone with baking soda. Label it BS.

6. Rinse the brush. Brush test a different zone with salt. Label it S.

NOTICE: What was the most effective cleaner? Did any of these cleaners scar the egg surface? Check with a magnifier. If you ran out of toothpaste, would you use salt or baking soda? Optional: Try a brush off test on the other side of the egg with a hard vs. soft toothbrush.

"BRUSHING IS SO BORING!"

And flossing is such a pain! Maybe losing a tooth or two in the far-off future is not such a bad trade-off? Think again. Having inflamed gums means having a constant, low-level infection. Your body is constantly fighting a war in your mouth. Unless you do something to beat back the attack, the microbes will continue to find new nooks and crannies to colonize. As their armies advance, your gums recede. Your body will have to expend more and more germ-fighting energy in a war it can't win.

Magnified used dental floss

THE HIGH COST OF WAR

The cure for plaque: Brush twice a day, floss once, and get regular cleanings.

Dogs too?

This fight can cost the loss of a tooth or teeth. More serious gum disease can open a door from your mouth into the bloodstream. This allows a constant shower of mouth microbes into your blood. Usually the body's defenses will quickly clear bacteria out of the blood. When a shower of bacteria turns into a flood, the body defenses can become overwhelmed. Over time your overall health can suffer.

UNHAPPY WANDERERS

Mouth microbes are constantly migrating to other parts of your body. Serious microbe infections in the mouth are associated with some surprising health effects. Sometimes mouth microbes migrate and become embedded in blood vessel walls. This can cause rough spots inside blood vessels. The result is hardening and thickening of the arteries. But that's not all. Serious gum infection is linked to an increased risk of heart attack and stroke. Women with mouth infections have a harder time getting pregnant, and infected gums have been linked to mothers giving birth to premature, low-weight babies.

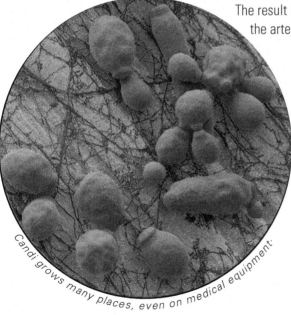

Candi grows many places, even on medical equipment.

FACT: Smokers are more prone to gum disease.

Chapter 4
PLAQUE TRACKING
Making Dead Mouths Talk

Keith Dobney studies old skulls. In 1980, he noticed that the ancient teeth in some skulls had tartar, just like modern teeth. Under a microscope, he could see dead microbes that had hardened into minerals, but he couldn't tell what kind they were. Years later, new DNA identification tools were invented that made it possible for Dobney and his team to go back and take a closer look.

Armed with the new tools, they probed the crud around the teeth of 34 skulls that ranged in age from 400 to 7,500 years old. Sorting the DNA in the plaque, Dobney's team now could identify exactly what types of bacteria had lived in these toothy scums. What they found was a surprise.

Our ancient ancestors had minimal tooth decay, despite the fact that it's highly unlikely they brushed. More recent teeth told a different story. These teeth had more plaque, more decay and more signs of gum disease. The scientists found the newer teeth had plenty of cavity-causing Mutans as well as bacteria associated with gum disease. These trouble-making bacteria were barely present on the older teeth but were much more plentiful on the younger ones. The scientists also noticed there was a later surge in cavities in the teeth from skulls from around 1800 – the century when sugar from the early American colonies starting flooding into Europe.

DNA "FINGERPRINTING"

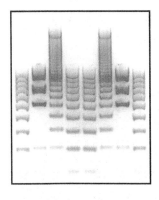

Have you ever noticed the barcodes on food labels that the grocery store cashier scans when you are checking out? Each code is a unique pattern of bars that allows the computer to identify each food item and how much it costs. Organisms also have unique patterns in their DNA, and scientists have developed ways to identify them. Patterns made by the unique DNA of each organism look almost like barcodes. Each unique pattern helps scientists identify each organism, whether living, dead or even extinct.

GUESS THEN TEST

Why would bacterial populations change over time? Why did the population of Mutans explode in modern mouths?

The researchers knew that humans started farming 10,000 years ago. Before then, humans dined on wild foods that are low in starch and sugars. Agriculture changed the human diet to mostly cereals.

Cereals are grasses that are grown for their edible seeds; they include wheat, corn and rice. Cereals are often high in starches and sugars. The scientists noticed that the deposits around the teeth of early farmers had far more carbohydrate-eating bacteria like Mutans that thrive on starches and sugars. The scientists hypothesized that cereal-based diets allowed cavity-causing mouth bacteria to flourish.

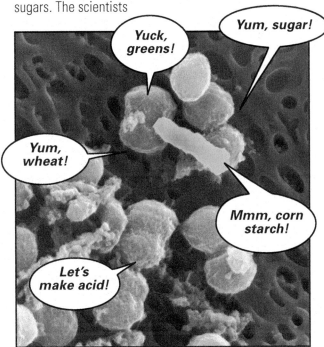

Colony of S. mutans

35

Streptococcus mutans:
aka: Mutans

DESCRIPTION Mutans are tough, sphere-shaped bacteria with thick outer walls made of protein and carbohydrates. Most live alone as a single cell, but they can also grow in long multi-cell chains that look like beads on a string.

HABITAT Mutans thrives in the human mouth. When scientists examine tooth cavities, they almost always find Mutans. Sometimes Mutans enters the bloodstream through wounds and spread to other parts of the body, where they can cause serious problems.

LIFESTYLE Mutans has evolved to live in the mouth, so it thrives at normal body temperature ($37°$ C or $98.6°$ F). It can live with or without oxygen, but grows faster when oxygen is present. Mutans has a double life. Sometimes it is a single-celled floater, drifting in your mouth's warm saliva.

Given an opportunity, it transforms itself into a sticker, settling into a biofilm anchored to a tooth.

SPECIAL TALENTS Mutans bacteria are table sugar junkies. Over the past 10,000 years, they evolved special sugar digesting powers to take advantage of humans' increasingly sweet and starchy diet. Mutans slurps up all kinds of sugar and can digest sucrose (table sugar), glucose (a sugar found in starchy plants), fructose (fruit sugar), and lactose (milk sugar). Sucrose is Mutans favorite food for making the sticky matrix materials in forming biofilms.

Mutans has acid-making habits. In the process of digesting sugars, it makes of a lot of an acid that dissolves tooth enamel. Until sugar flooded our diet, Mutans lived with humans without doing much harm. In fact, Mutans and other bacteria that live in the mouth help boost our immune system and prevent more dangerous microbes from colonizing our mouths.

FAMILY NEWS On the tree of life, Mutans belongs to the family Streptococcaceae, which is a big group of bacteria. More than twenty of Mutans' cousins can live in your mouth. Some strains of Mutans are not a problem for humans, while others are.

FACT: Surprisingly, 10% of people with serious tooth decay don't carry any Mutans bacteria.

ANOTHER APPROACH
Making Mutations Count

Another team of scientists looked into modern mouths and harvested DNA from Mutans bacteria from people currently living in different parts of the world. They analyzed the DNA from the ancient Mutans and compared it to the DNA of modern Mutans. Scientists know that DNA mutates over time, and they can estimate the rate at which mutations occur. By counting the differences between the DNA in ancient Mutans and the DNA of modern Mutans, the researchers estimated how long ago the Mutans genome (the full set of all the DNA in an organism) started to change.

These scientists discovered that Mutans bacteria started changing about 10,000 years ago. They also observed that changes to Mutans genes had to do with Mutans' ability to convert sugar to energy. Thus, Mutans started having changes in its DNA that allowed it to more efficiently turn sugars into energy, and it developed a tolerance for living in an acidic environment. This occurred at the same time that humans started farming cereal plants and eating more of these grains.

Humans who lived before 10,000 years ago ate a mix of wild foods.

Farmers' diets 5,000 years ago switched to much more grain.

Modern diets have increasing amounts of sugar.

WHAT CAN WE LEARN HERE?

So, what do ancient skulls have to do with you and your mouth? If you ate a diet of raw grains and almost no sugar, your mouth bacteria might not have enough fuel to make acid. The more recent human diet of refined sugars and starches started wreaking havoc on human teeth about 10,000 years ago, and our resident mouth microbes adapted to this dietary change.

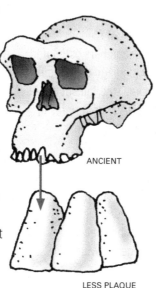

ANCIENT

LESS PLAQUE

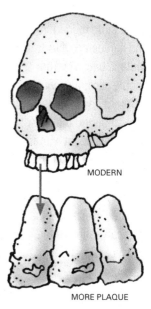

MODERN

MORE PLAQUE

ACID TIME

Ready, Set, Go!

Did you know it's healthier for your teeth if you eat a pound of sugar once a day than if you sip sugary drinks all day long? OK, eating a whole pound of sugar is a bad idea. But a quick sugar shower is better for you teeth than an all-day soaking. That's because every sugary soda or sweet snack or starchy nibble you chew feeds your acid-making bacteria. After eating these foods, the bacteria continue to acidify your mouth for about 20 minutes.

Activity: The Acid Time Test

How much time are your teeth in the destructive acid zone every day? It's easy to estimate. Think back. Add up your sweet snacks and drinks for an average day and night, then multiply by 20 minutes. Voila! Acid attack time.

Acid Attack Time Tally	Example	Your numbers here
1. Number of sweet snacks in a day.	4	
2. Number of sweet drinks in a day.	1	
3. Add up snacks and drinks (1 and 2)	5	
4. Multiply snack and drink total x 20 mins.	100	
Total number of acid attack minutes:	100 minutes	
5. Add minutes spent sipping/snacking	60 minutes	
Total Daily Acid Attack Time	160 minutes	

If you are a soda sipper or a candy sucker there is more bad news, because your teeth are affected for a longer time. For example, if you sip on a soda for an hour, the acid attacks would go on for that whole hour plus 20 minutes after your last sip. That's 90 minutes of acid attack in total! (You might want to go back and adjust your total with some extra sipping time.)

Go ahead. Guess how many teaspoons of sugar are in a 12-ounce can of cola.

HOW SWEET IS IT?

The answer is about ten. Maybe you're thinking, "So what? What's a few extra sugar calories in the diet of a busy kid like me?" Instead of thinking of sugar as quick energy, think of it as bacteria snacks ... an energy supply for powering acid attacks on your teeth. Just for fun, add up how many teaspoons of sugar you feed your mouth microbes on an average day.

Activity: Sugar Scout

Is sugar a towering presence in your diet? Think not? Here's an experiment that will show you how sugar stacks up in your diet.

YOU NEED:
- a box of sugar cubes or a bowl of sugar
- some of your food favorites (with nutrition labels)
- 12 saucers or napkins
- measuring spoon (if using table sugar)

Part 1: Sugar Scouting

1. Gather up at least six of your food favorites. Guess which foods have the most and the least sugar.

2. Measure one serving of each food onto a saucer or napkin.

Damage control is possible!

Eat fewer sweets!

More meat?

Chew sugarless gum!

Always rinse after snacks!

Wow!

many cubes worth of sugar lives in a serving size.) If you're using table sugar, 1 teaspoon of sugar = 4 grams.

6. Count out the sugar spoons or cubes and put them next to the food sample. (It's OK to round up.)

7. Do this for each of your foods. Any surprises?

NOTICE: If you want to really be surprised, check out the sugar in these foods: Raisins, dried fruits, soda, graham crackers, spaghetti sauce, and snack yogurts.

3. To find out the size of a serving for that food, read the Nutrition Facts label on the package.

4. To find out how many grams of sugar is lurking in the food, read the label. Go down the list until you find Total Carbohydrate. Sugars are listed here in grams.

5. Divide the total sugar grams by 4. (One sugar cube equals 4 grams, so this math tells you how

Part 2: Sweet Quiz

Now it's time to have some fun with your sugar exhibit. Scramble the samples. Invite a friend or family member to test their sugar savvy by matching the sugar piles to the foods.

Chapter 5

SPIT

Your Mouth's Miracle Fluid

Most people don't think about much about saliva, unless it happens to escape their lips. Then it becomes spit, a vile liquid you may want to apologize for. In fact, saliva is a highly under-rated, multi-purpose liquid.

SPIT: WHAT IS IT?

Mostly water. Saliva is about 99% water, plus small amounts of dissolved minerals such as fluoride, calcium and phosphate. You have your own personal mix of spit minerals. Saliva also contains some proteins, enzymes and a number of antimicrobial substances. Also floating around in your spit are a lot of sloughed off dead cheek cells, vast numbers of free-floating microbes and an even vaster number of bacteria-killing viruses called bacteriophages.

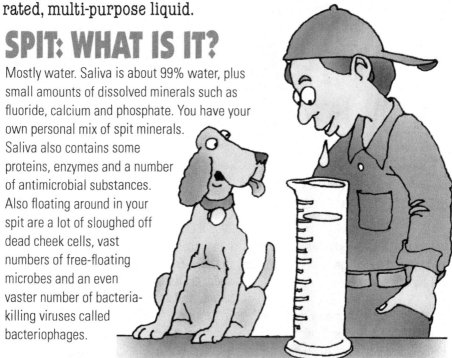

FIRST AID FOR TEETH

Humble saliva does a number of jobs. One of its jobs is keeping your teeth safe. Your spit dilutes some of the harmful chemicals (even natural substances like sugar or lemon juice are technically chemicals) that you put in your mouth as you eat and drink your way throughout the day. Not only does it weaken acids that can damage your teeth, spit has restorative powers. It can replace some minerals in your teeth after an acid attack.

SALIVA:
THE GREAT LUBRICATOR

Think of your mouth as a smash compactor for food, equipped with 32 shredders and grinders called teeth. Your teeth take whole foods and efficiently grind them to a pulp that is mixed with your digesting chemicals. Saliva squirts into your mouth, while the tongue mixes the food mass around, packing chewed food into a ball that is easy to swallow. If you swallow food that is too bulky or dry there is a real danger of choking. Choking can kill you.

Saliva doesn't just save your life, it saves the inside of your mouth. Chomping and chewing creates a lot of friction, giving the cells lining your mouth and gums a real beating. Rips and cuts in the oral cavity are an open invitation to germs. Slippery saliva lessens friction and smooths the way so the surfaces inside your mouth don't get torn.

Spit is good stuff – a miracle fluid in many ways.

YUCK! SPIT

"But spit is nasty," you're thinking. Actually, it has many microbe-fighting substances and some very interesting properties. Saliva is home base to a lot of microbes, most of which are harmless. Nonetheless, it's a good idea to keep spit to yourself and not turn the world into your spittoon.

MOUTH WATERING
Saliva's Source

Every day your body makes between 1 and 2 quarts of saliva. Where does it all come from? Three sets of hard-working salivary glands do the job of keeping your mouth constantly watered. One set lies beneath the tongue, another is in the jaws near your bottom molars, and a third set is beside the ears on the inside of the cheeks. Another 800 tiny glands dot the inside of your mouth. All these glands are connected by ducts that dump a constant flow of spit into your mouth.

Wow! Two quarts is a half gallon.

SALIVA, THICK AND THIN

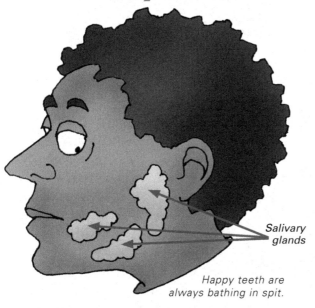

Salivary glands

Happy teeth are always bathing in spit.

FACT: *Saliva contains calcium and phosphate. These minerals in your saliva help to repair the microscopic dings on the surface of your teeth.*

You have not one, but two types of saliva.

Thin saliva makes up about 80% of your daily supply. Thin saliva is what you feel rushing into your mouth when you're really hungry and you smell food. Thin saliva flows into your mouth from the big glands between your ear and cheek.

Thick saliva makes up the rest of your daily spit production. This kind is built to stick to teeth. It coats teeth with substances that help repair the damage to your tooth enamel after an acid attack.

Activity: Mouth-Watering Fun

Want to feel your salivary glands at work? Here's how to instantly turn them on so you can feel a gush of saliva flooding your mouth.

YOU NEED:
• a slice of lemon or lime

1. Stick your tongue out of your mouth.

2. Pay attention while you rub the citrus slice on the tip of your tongue.

3. Describe the feelings in your mouth.

Taste buds are 30% less sensitive in the dry air of an airplane cabin. Saliva makes food seem tastier.

NOTICE: Did you feel a sensation of liquid flooding your mouth? When your tongue senses the acid in the lemon or lime, your brain gets the message and instantly turns on your saliva glands. This flood of saliva dilutes the acid you just put in your mouth and protects your teeth.

SALIVA: The Liquifier

Ever notice that dry foods aren't as tasty? Saliva turns foods into liquids. When food is made liquid, your digestive chemicals work better. Also, liquid foods flow into the nooks and crannies of the tongue so your taste buds can better sense what you are eating.

Your tongue is a chemical sensor. One of its jobs is to prevent you from swallowing something bad. Your taste buds sense food as it washes over the tongue. Nerves in the taste buds relay the information to your brain. The brain analyzes the information and quickly sends out command messages like: "Time to swallow." "Yum, is there more?" "YUCK! ROTTEN! SPIT NOW!!!" "Uh oh. Too dry. More saliva to mouth."

Close-up of taste bud

Close-up of tongue bumps

Treponema denticola
aka: Denti

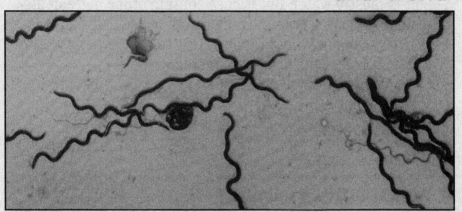

DESCRIPTION

Denti are long, flexible, spiral-shaped bacteria belonging to a group called spirochetes. They swim easily through fluids with a twisting motion. This talent helps them find their way under your gums.

HABITAT

Denti are often found in the human mouth. They like to live in the pockets under the gums where they thrive in low-oxygen environments. Denti grows best at normal body temperature (37º C, or 98.6º F).

FACT: *Flossing is a great tool for removing irritating plaque. One survey found only about 13% of Americans floss daily. Make your teeth happy, do it every day.*

FACT: *Many types of long, spiral-shaped bacteria (aka spirochetes) live in the human mouth.*

LIFESTYLE

Denti join the biofilm community once it is well established. They dine on a clear liquid that oozes from irritated gums. Denti are often found with a couple of their buddy microbes in a tooth-threatening gang called "The Red Complex."

SPECIAL TALENTS

Denti are good at digesting proteins. One of their survival tricks is to stop some of the body's immune cells.

Big numbers of wiggly Denti are a sign of gum disease. Plaque deposits containing Denti irritate the gums. If left in place, this triggers inflammation that destroys the gum and bone tissue that hold your teeth in place. This disease is called periodontitis.

Activity: Spit Stretch Test

Spit is mostly water. But it does contain other ingredients, including tangles of long, thin protein molecules. Saliva is sticky because of these tangles. Test to see how sticky and elastic it is by comparing it to water.

YOU NEED:
- a ruler (one marked in centimeters works best)
- a paper cup of water
- pencil and paper

Part 1: Saliva vs. Water

1. Run your forefinger along your gums to collect a drop of saliva.

2. Put the drop of saliva between your thumb and forefinger. Slowly pull your fingers apart so the saliva forms a strand.

2. Observe what happens.

3. Measure the length of the strand. Record your observations

4. Now try the test with a drop of water.

5. Repeat the test three more times for each liquid.

6. What did you notice? Record your observations. How far can you stretch spit vs. water?

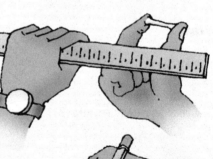

	Spit stretch length in centimeters	Water stretch length in centimeters
Test 1		
Test 2		
Test 3		
Test 4		
Observations: (How are water and spit different?)		

NOTICE: Water has a tiny bit of stretch. You know this if you have ever tried to pull a drop of water apart. Water wants to stick to itself. This is called "surface tension." However, the long protein molecules in saliva make it very sticky and stretchy. These qualities allow it to stick to your tooth surfaces and act as a lubricant.

Activity: The Spit Stretch Challenge

How far can you go? With a little practice you can get your spit to stretch an amazing length. Why waste this talent? Challenge a friend to a stretch race.

YOU NEED:
- a ruler (marked in centimeters)
- a friend
- pencil and paper

1. Show your friend how to stretch spit.

2. Give your friend a few minutes to practice.

3. Decide on how many trials and how you will record the results.

4. Ready, set, stretch!

5. Record the results. The longest stretch wins.

THE AMAZING MAGNIFIED STRETCH

Look closely at a strand of stretched spit and you will see something surprising. Beads appear on the strand after a few seconds. What you are seeing is the long protein molecules stretching while the water part of spit forms beads along the strand. To see this effect clearly, stretch the spit against a dark background with a strong side light. Use a magnifier to see more detail.

Your Results:	Spit stretch length in centimeters	Friend's Results:	Spit stretch length in centimeters
Test 1		Test 1	
Test 2		Test 2	
Test 3		Test 3	
Test 4		Test 4	
Test 5		Test 5	
Winning stretch			
Observations: (what worked, what didn't?)		Observations: (what worked, what didn't?)	

NOTICE: Does stretch speed affect the result? Does the amount of saliva affect the result? Do you think everybody's saliva has equal stretch?

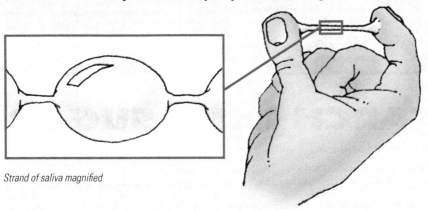

Strand of saliva magnified

SALIVA: THE GREAT DIGESTER

A number of chemical reactions happen just behind your smile. The first steps at turning breakfast toast into usable nutrients happen in the mouth. After your shredders mash your food to a pulp, saliva provides breakdown chemicals called enzymes.

Enzymes are substances that your body makes that act like chemical knives. They cut complex food bits into simpler materials your body can use. Saliva contains a number of enzymes. Protease breaks apart proteins. Lipase breaks down fats. Amylase takes apart carbohydrates, turning them into simpler sugars. All this digesting happens before your food even arrives in your stomach.

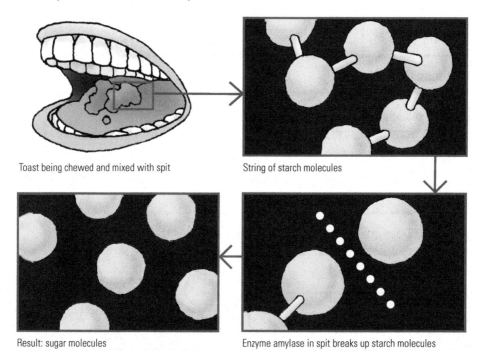

Toast being chewed and mixed with spit

String of starch molecules

Result: sugar molecules

Enzyme amylase in spit breaks up starch molecules

STARCH INTO SUGAR

Starch is a major ingredient of carbohydrate foods like bread and crackers. Starch is made of long chains of individual sugars linked together. Amylase is an enzyme that cuts a starch chain, clipping it back into individual sugars. Starch has a nonsweet flavor. Sugar tastes sweet. You can actually taste amylase working in your mouth changing starch into sugars.

Activity: Tasting Enzyme Action

Taste the powers of the starch-digesting enzyme, amylase, as it performs its amazing work of carbohydrate breakdown. Spit supplies the enzyme; all you need is a starchy cracker.

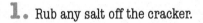

YOU NEED:
• a soda cracker (unsalted saltines are best)

1. Rub any salt off the cracker.

2. Taste the soda cracker with the tip of your tongue. Notice the taste of starch before it is worked on by saliva.

3. Take a few bites out of the cracker. Give them a couple of chews.

4. Hold those bites on the tip of your tongue for a minute or two. Don't swallow.

5. Pay attention. What's happening to the cracker? What do you feel and taste?

6. After about two minutes describe what's left of the cracker. Compare the taste of the dry cracker to the saliva soaked bits. Now you can swallow.

NOTICE: Did the cracker turn from dry to wet? Did you also notice a flow of saliva into your mouth and into the cracker turning it from stiff to soggy? Were you able to taste the cracker getting sweeter? That's the work of the enzyme amylase breaking starch into sugar.

WASHDAY MIRACLE

Did you know that laundry detergent contains some of same digestive chemicals that are found in the human body? Modern detergent is a potion of stain digesters, including some of the enzymes found in your saliva: amylase for breaking down starch, lipase for attacking fats and proteases for busting up proteins. Credit for this novel use of enzymes goes to a German chemist, Otto Rohm, who tested the powers of these digestive chemicals. He wondered, if these chemicals could break down grass in a cow's stomach, why wouldn't they break down grass stains on a pair of pants? He tested his hunch by collecting digestive juices from cow pancreases (an organ in mammals that makes important digestive enzymes, among other things). His experiments were a success; and as a result, today we all live a more stain-free life. Pulverized cow pancreases proved too expensive. Today enzymes for our laundry detergents are grown in the lab with the help of a special type of fungus.

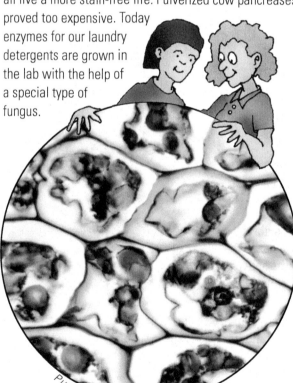

Purple starch stains in potato cells

YOU NEED:
- 2 soda crackers (aka saltine)
- 4 clear, small glasses
- table sugar
- iodine (tincture of iodine from the medicine cabinet or drug store)
- an eyedropper
- a teaspoon
- a black marker
- a plate

Part 1: The Test for Starch

1. Put a few drops of iodine in a glass. Add a teaspoon of water.

2. Hold it up to the light. You will see the color is light brown.

3. Put a drop of this diluted iodine directly onto a cracker.

NOTICE: If the iodine turns blue-black on the cracker it means starch is present.

Activity: Tattletale Color

A chemical indicator is a tattletale chemical that changes color in the presence of a particular substance. Iodine is one of these tattletales. A drop of brown iodine turns blue-black in the presence of starch. You can use iodine to prove that your saliva has the power to turn starch into sugar.

Pinch of Sugar

2 tsp Water

Pinch of Cracker

2 tsp Water

Pinch of Cracker

1 tsp Water + 1 tsp Spit

1 Drop Iodine Each

Part 2: Test for Enzyme Action

1. Put a soda cracker on a plate. Grind it into fine dust with the back of a spoon.

2. Set out the other three glasses.

3. Put a pinch of sugar in one glass. Add two teaspoons of water. Label it A with the marker.

4. Put a pinch of soda cracker dust into each of the other two glasses.

5. Add two teaspoons of water to one of these two glasses. Label it B.

6. Add one teaspoon of water and one teaspoon of spit to the third glass. Label it C.

7. Let the glasses sit for ten minutes. Give each a stir with a clean spoon to help them dissolve.

8. Add a drop or two of iodine to each glass. Watch what happens.

NOTICE: Where did you find starch present? Where was it missing? How do you explain what happened in each cup?

SPIT: GERM TRAPPER

Not only is your saliva chock full of germ-fighting substances, it is also a germ trap. Its stickiness can surround microbes, capturing them in salivary goo. When you swallow, this goo slides down your throat. Microbes are flushed into the stomach, where they die in a pit of acid. Few germs survive the trip.

Viruses escaping from dying strep bacteria

In all watery ecosystems where there are bacteria, there are predatory viruses that attack and kill bacteria. Most of these viruses are known as bacteriophages (bacteria eaters). In the ocean there are about a thousand viral particles for every microbe. This is also true in your mouth!

DROOL?

So why do dogs and babies drool? Drool happens when you lose control of the muscles of your mouth and jaw. Little babies haven't gained control of their mouth muscles yet, plus they don't have teeth to dam the flow. Like dogs, babies have no shame, so they don't really care if they drool.

Eeeew! Dog drool!

Eeeew! Human drool!

SPIT

ANTIMICROBIAL AGENT

Your mouth is a major gateway to an outside world teeming with potential microbes that can cause you harm. It's a natural place for your body to post some frontline defenses. Your spit is well armed with germ-fighting chemicals. Your body makes a range of different homegrown antimicrobial agents for fending off bad bugs – many of the proteins floating in your saliva are dedicated to microbe control. Each has its own trick for fending off harmful microbes. Here is a small sample of some of them:

LYSOZYME specializes in digesting the cell walls of some bacteria. You can find lysozyme in fluids that are exposed to lots of bugs, like saliva, tears, earwax and mucus. ("Bugs" is scientist slang for microbes.)

PEROXIDASE turns the waste products made by bacteria into a chemical weapon, then it uses this weapon against the bacteria to limit their growth.

MUCIN is a super sticky salivary material that lubricates your mouth, helping prevent sores. It also fights microbes.

LACTOFERRIN interferes with stickiness of bacteria so they can't form biofilms. It also gloms onto many microbes, and it can limit the growth of viruses, fungi and bacteria.

SECRETORY IgA is salivary protein that acts as a glommer, sticking to many bugs and trapping them in saliva. You swallow the trapped bugs, which are then swept into the acid bath in your stomach. It is important, but not the only sticky trick in your body's defenses.

Chapter 6

DEATH BREATH

Stinky Bacteria & Halitosis

Ever wake up in the morning with a bad taste and the sense that something died in your mouth during the night? Did you have that fuzzy teeth feeling? Nasty breath? While you were sleeping, the microbes in your mouth were growing wild: digesting, fermenting and decomposing bits of left-behind organic materials.

Why the late-night microbe frenzy? Your oral habitat changes in your sleep: The constant gush of daytime saliva slows to a trickle. The swishing action of your tongue slows down during a nap. Open-mouthed snoozing dries the mouth. The microbes that colonize the surfaces of your teeth thrive with less washing action.

Forget to brush? Sleeping with a dirty mouth leaves behind lots of food bits for your microbes to feast on. More food and less liquid turbulence give your mouth microbes a boost. That bad taste and smell in your mouth is proof your mouth microbes were alive and thriving while you slept.

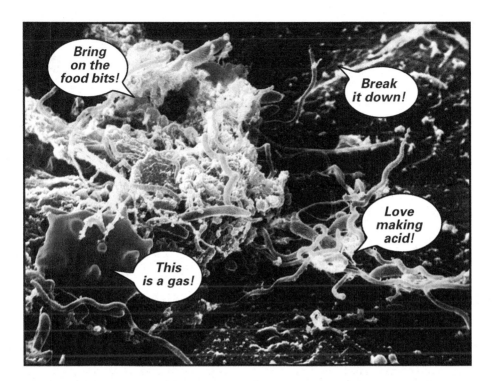

DIGESTION VS. FERMENTATION

Digestion is breaking down the food you eat into usable parts – recycling at its best. As food passes through our digestive system, our teeth mash and crush food into smaller bits. These pieces are still way too big to be absorbed into your bloodstream and sent throughout your body, but digestive enzymes are really good at breaking food into smaller pieces that can be reused wherever they are needed in your body.

It's like building with bricks. You can build a lot of different things with bricks, but you need to start with the basic building blocks. Food is made up of lots of building blocks that can be used many ways in your body. Digestion breaks the food down into its individual bricks, so that these bricks can be recombined to build something your body needs, like new hair, skin or tooth enamel.

Fermentation is a special kind of sugar digestion. It breaks down sugars into acids and gases. The products of fermentation are acid (vinegar) and alcohol (in beer or wine). The gases are carbon dioxide (the bubbles in soda water) or hydrogen (one ingredient in farts). Bacteria use fermentation – both inside your body and out. Humans have figured out how to use bacterial fermentation to make pickles and yogurt.

Halitosis

Legend tells us an advertising company coined the word halitosis for bad breath in the 1920s to sell mouthwash. But halitosis has been in the English language for about 200 years. Halitosis derives from a Latin word, *halitus* (breath), and a Greek word, *osis* (terrible condition). The smell of bad breath has been around for as long as humans have had bacteria in their mouths. That's about the same amount of time that humans have had mouths!

Thy breath stinketh...

Cheers! To sweet breath.

BANISHING THE Bad

Humans have been fighting bad breath for thousands of years. They've invented many remedies. The ancient Greek physician Hippocrates advised a mouth rinse of red wine and spices. Chinese visitors to court were required to chew a clove before speaking to their emperor.

DOUBLE BAD

Phew! Park those somewhere else!

Experts divide bad breath into two types. Temporary bad breath is when you burp burger or exhale a whiff of onion. These foul smells are the short-term result of something you recently ate. Some of the substances in foods you eat release chemicals into your blood stream and these are picked up by the breath as it is exhaled from the lungs. The good news is this goes away rapidly.

Chronic bad breath stays around. It has many causes, including smoking, mouth infections, chronic sinus drip, diseases like cancer, medications that cause dry mouth, and tonsil stones. Sometimes a broken filling can trap food particles that decay and stink. Not brushing your teeth can give you a case of chronic bad breath. A common cause of bad breath is bacteria that hang out in the furry pockets at the back of the tongue.

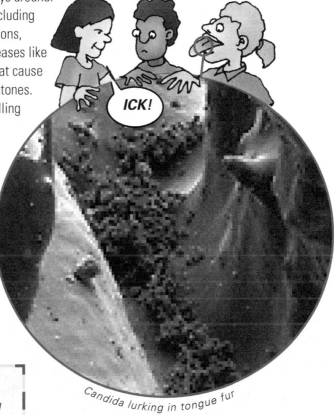

ICK!

Candida lurking in tongue fur

FACT: *According to old Jewish law, bad breath was grounds for divorce.*

WHAT'S UP?

Parking tiny cars or jellybeans up the nose can cause bad breath. Who would do such a weird thing? When a toddler has bad breath, the Mayo Clinic suggests looking up the kid's nose. A toy car up the nose of a toddler can lead to changes in the microbes. It acts like an infection, causing the nose bacteria to produce bad-smelling sulfur compounds. This nose air reaches the back of the throat and can become part of a kid's exhaled breath. (You might have noticed the nose-throat connection during a laughing fit when milk squirts out of your nose.)

61

MY TONGUE HAS FUR?

Open wide, glance inside and notice the top surface of your tongue. At first glance it looks like a fuzzy pink carpet. Look more closely and you can see individual bumps. On closer inspection you will observe that these bumps are not created equal. There are three types of bumps:

Small round bumps are equipped with taste buds. These sensors taste sweet, salty, bitter, sour and "umami" (a savory flavor).

Big round bumps are surrounded by a deep ridge. They also have taste buds.

Spikey bumps grip food and sense heat, cold, touch and pain. They can sense the fire of hot peppers but they can't taste.

TONGUE MAP:
- ROOT
- Taste buds
- BODY
- Papillae
- TIP

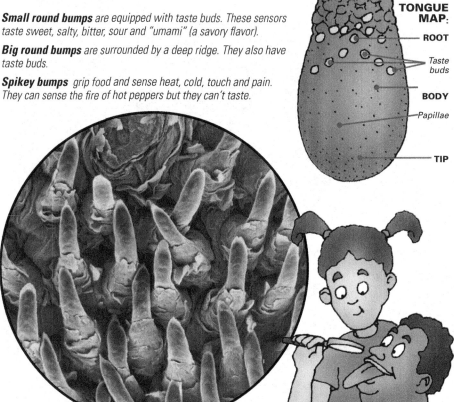

Tongue surface magnified

The underside of the tongue looks completely different, with thin, see-through tissue. Here you will find:

- **Veins**: Big blue blood vessels that return blood to the heart.
- **Capillaries**: Tiny, red vessels that supply oxygen and food to the tongue tissues.
- **Frenulum**: A flap of skin that attaches the tongue to the bottom of the mouth.
- **Salivary glands**: The biggest saliva glands in your mouth are found on either side of the frenulum.

Activity: Tongue Check

Look closely at your tongue. For most people the tongue is unknown territory. You will probably find some surprising lumps and bumps.

YOU NEED:
- a mirror
- a good light source
- a tongue depressor
  (a clean popsicle stick
  works fine)

1. Take a good look at your tongue using a mirror in a good light.

2. Use the depressor to push the tongue around to get a good look.

3. Notice the underside of your tongue is smooth and slippery. Cells here form a thin uniform skin, so transparent that you can clearly see the tongue's blood vessels.

4. The top side of your tongue is textured and pink. This is the surface that looks furry.

NOTICE: Use a magnifier to look closely. Can you find the different types of tongue bumps? Is the top different from the underside? Does the front look different than the back?

BAD NEWS AT THE BACK OF THE TONGUE

Marcello Riggio, a scientist with a special interest in bad-breath bacteria, zeroes in on the microbes that colonize the back of the tongue. He found that most tongues host similar microbes, but each person differs in how many of each kind of microbe. He found people with bad breath have higher numbers of smell-producing microbes. Even if they are fanatic brushers and flossers, they can still spew stinky breath.

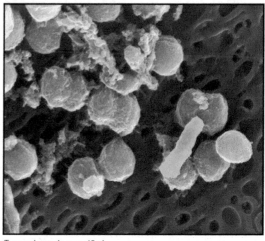
Tongue bacteria magnified

WHAT TO DO?

There is less chance of having bad breath if you can reduce the number of bacteria at the rear of your tongue. Bad breath bacteria are buried deep within the tongue "fur". Giving the rear of the tongue a regular scrub will knock down the bacterial population and sweeten up your breath.

Magnified tongue surface

TONGUE SCRAPING

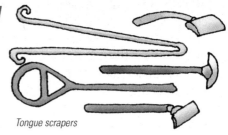

Tongue scraping is a popular activity in India where it is common to clean your tongue as well as your teeth. A special tool makes it easy to open wide and slide the accumulated biofilm off your tongue.

Tongue scrapers

Activity: Tongue Scrape

If you don't believe gunk stacks up on your tongue "fur" try using your fingernail as a scraper.

YOU NEED:
- a mirror
- a good light source
- clean hands

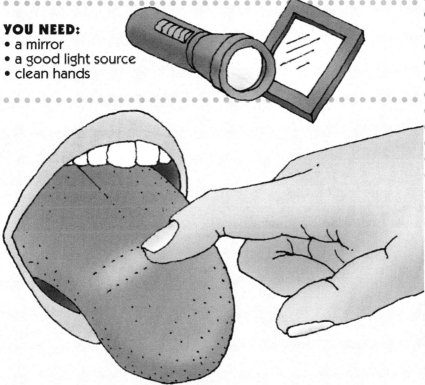

1. Wash your hands well, and clean your nails.

2. Open wide in front of a mirror. A strong light helps.

3. Reach towards the back of the tongue and gently rub your nail across the surface.

NOTICE: Check your tongue again. Notice any difference where you scraped? Notice anything under your fingernail? Why do you think some dentists recommend brushing your tongue as well as your teeth?

WHAT STINKS?

There are zillions of cells dead and alive floating around in your mouth right now. Even a pea-sized bit of spit contains millions of microbes. All of these tiny life forms take in food and excrete leftovers. As many as 150 different molecules may be made by mouth microbes as they break down foods. Some of these broken-down substances really stink.

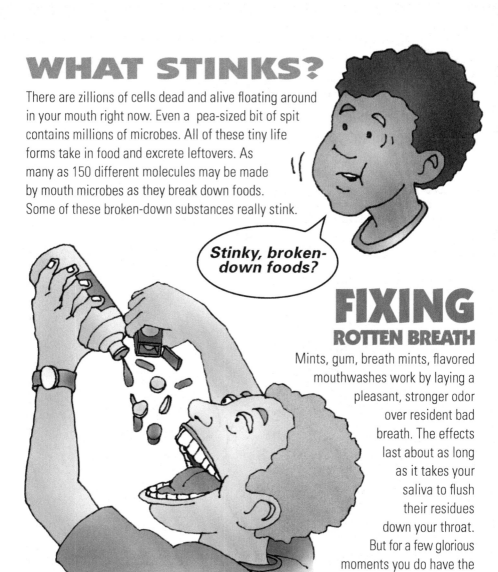

Stinky, broken-down foods?

FIXING
ROTTEN BREATH

Mints, gum, breath mints, flavored mouthwashes work by laying a pleasant, stronger odor over resident bad breath. The effects last about as long as it takes your saliva to flush their residues down your throat. But for a few glorious moments you do have the feeling that "Yes! I'm getting the upper hand on my nasty breath." It doesn't fix the problem. It just puts a mask on it.

COVER-UPS

Humans spend millions on making their breath sweeter. Mouthwash ads suggest bad breath will leave you friendless, jobless and in the gutter. All sorts of potions and rinses promise better breath. Do they work? That depends on what you mean by "work."

FACT: *Urine was a common ingredient of mouthwash until the 18th century.*

Surely all those powerful mouthwashes with the reassuring bacteria-killing claims do the job? Yes, they do kill mouth bacteria, anywhere from about 20 minutes to a few hours. But then all the bacteria rebound. Unfortunately, these chemicals kill the good bacteria as well as bad. Alcohol, the bacterial control liquid in many mouthwashes, dries the mouth. A dry mouth actually helps microbes thrive.

KILLER CHEMICALS

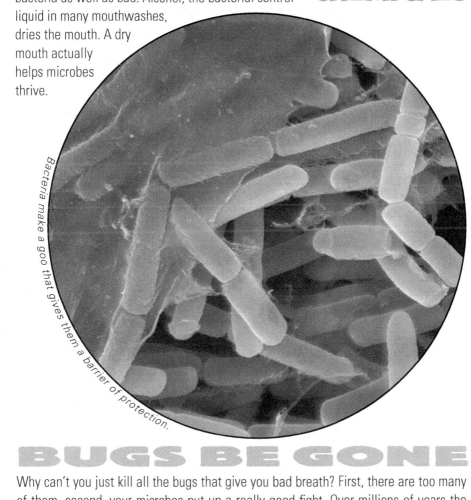

Bacteria make a goo that gives them a barrier of protection.

BUGS BE GONE

Why can't you just kill all the bugs that give you bad breath? First, there are too many of them, second, your microbes put up a really good fight. Over millions of years the microbes have developed all sorts of tricks for avoiding your body's defenses. Biofilms are thick. Most medicines and mouthwashes can't penetrate a biofilm to kill germs that live there. Some mouth bacteria can evade detection by wearing a crystalline invisibility cloak. Others can shut down our killer defense cells. Others can disappear into our body's cells and hide out. Even if a microbe doesn't have an effective defense it can often get one with a trick called "resistance."

Candida albicans:
aka: Candi

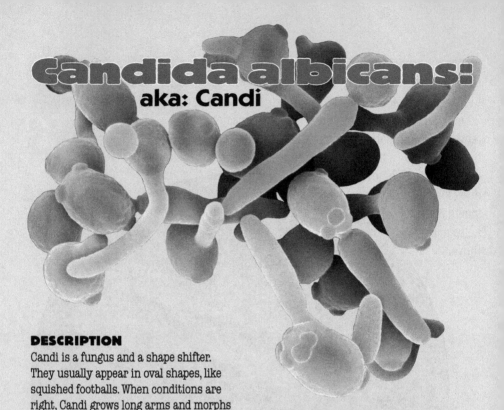

DESCRIPTION
Candi is a fungus and a shape shifter. They usually appear in oval shapes, like squished footballs. When conditions are right, Candi grows long arms and morphs into a mean-looking hyphal form.

HABITAT
Candi is a normal resident in most everybody's mouth, throat, gut, genital tract and skin. Candi usually lives peacefully in humans without causing harm.

LIFESTYLE
Candi loves sugar. This tough little yeast feasts on carbohydrates in your mouth and gut. Unlike many microbes in your mouth, Candi is a fungus, not a bacterium. Drugs that control bacteria have no effect on these fungi. After taking antibiotics, humans sometimes develop an infection that looks like a white coating on the throat or tongue. That's because the antibiotics wiped out the bacterial competition and created a space for Candi to grow wild. This is a yeast infection called "thrush."

SPECIAL TALENTS
In healthy people, Candi gets by without being noticed, feasting on the excess sugar in our diets. If the population of Candi gets too big in a healthy person, the body's defenses go to work and usually bring it under control. However, in a sick person, Candi can be serious. In a person with a weak immune system, it can undergo a personality change. Candi changes shape and grows long tendrils called hyphae. These sticky hyphae can grow into lungs, kidneys, brains and blood vessels, making a person seriously sick.

FAMILY NEWS
Candi is a member of the fungus clan and a cousin of molds and mushrooms.

> **FACT:** *Candi are more abundant in the mouths of people with pierced tongues.*

WEAPONS SHARING

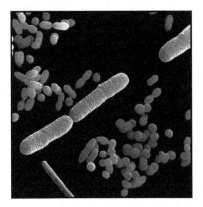

When a biofilm is exposed to a killer mouthwash, some of the bacteria will die, but many of the bugs will live. These bacteria, immune to mouthwashes, will continue to make copies of themselves. We call these microbes "resistant." These survivor microbes have DNA that codes for resistance to the chemicals in the mouthwashes. These bacteria are able to share their resistance genes by passing them around to other members of the community. Eventually, the whole biofilm becomes resistant. This weapons-sharing activity is called "gene swapping."

GENE SWAPPING

Bacteria regularly swap genes that give them new abilities and sometimes even "superpowers" like antibiotic resistance. Different kinds of microbes can swap genes, making them hard to kill. Also, some bacteria can reproduce every 20 minutes. Because there are so many of them swapping genetic material so often, their chances of hitting the jackpot with a new killer weapon is pretty good. This is how bacteria regularly evolve ways to disarm antibiotics and all the antibacterial substances that humans launch at them.

Activity: Breath Secrets

Bad breath? Mint to the rescue! In the United States we put mint in gum, embed it in after dinner candies, put it in mouth rinses. Mint is the custom in America, but it is not the only breath freshener. In India people finish a meal by chewing mukhawaas, a mix of aromatic fennel seeds. Cloves sweeten breath in China. Every culture has its own ways of dealing with halitosis.

Survey people you know to find out their secrets for sweet breath. It's especially fun to ask people from other countries. Here are some sample questions:

What do you do when you have bad breath?
Do you know any special home remedies for halitosis?
What did your grandparents do to keep their breath sweet?

Chapter 7

TONSILS

Tonsil Stones & Secrets of the Crypts

Kissing, licking and sticking things in your mouth are all invitations to microbes to come on board your body. It's only natural that your body has some front-line defenses to block invading organisms. You have defenders in your mouth and throat called tonsils.

Defenders in my throat?

TONSILS: WHAT GOOD ARE THEY?

Your tonsils are part of your body's immune system and are home to white blood cells that are always on patrol for microbe invaders. Two masses of spongy tissue make up

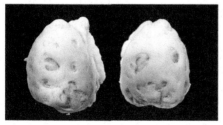

the tonsils that stand guard in your throat just behind your tongue. Average tonsils measure about an inch wide by an inch and a half long, though some people have been known to have tonsils twice this size.

Tonsil stones

70

GERM TRAPS

People used to think of tonsils as germ filters. Unlucky microbes that wandered into the tonsils were promptly attacked and digested by the resident white blood cells hanging out in the tonsil tissues. Now scientists think of tonsils as a finely tuned surveillance system. They are on constant alert and stay ready to respond to any new microbial pests that invade the mouth.

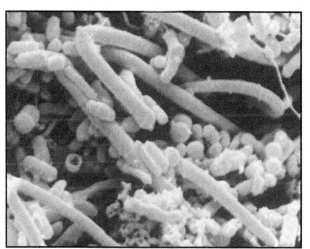

Bacteria in inflamed tonsils

IN THE CRYPTS:
TONSIL FUNCTIONS

The tonsils in your throat are basically a mass of immune cells with folds and creases called crypts. These deep creases provide lots of surface area for bacterial contact. A biofilm community of resident microbes colonizes these crypts. The surveillance cells in the tonsils are OK with these on-board bugs. The resident microbes are recognized and tolerated by the immune system, but when something new and strange comes along, the body attacks the foreign bugs.

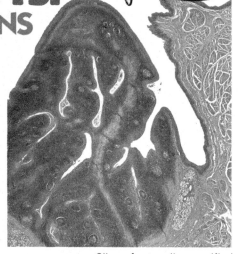

CRYPT.

Slice of a tonsil, magnified

GAG RESPONSE

Tonsil probing can be tricky. Did you notice that as you press down on the back of the tongue, you suddenly feel your stomach heave? This is the gag response. Your mouth and throat are wired to automatically reject anything being forced into the throat. This choke protection is great for keeping the airways clear, but it's a problem for tonsil gazers. There are some gag prevention tricks. Try making a tight fist, or humming, or putting a dab of salt on your tongue.

How DOES he do that?

RING OF TONSILS

You have more tonsils than meet the eye. In fact, you have a whole group of these protector tissues in the mouth. Another pair of tissues guard your nasal passages. And you have even more tonsil tissue on the back of the tongue.

Together these tissues form what is sometimes called the tonsillar ring, a set of well-placed defenses around your nose, throat and mouth.

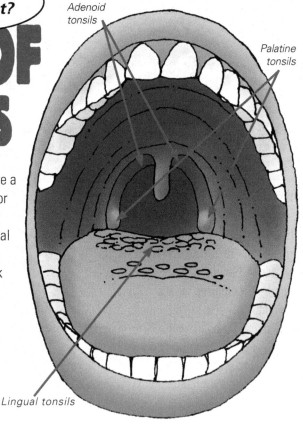

Adenoid tonsils

Palatine tonsils

Lingual tonsils

Activity: Tonsil Diving

Unless you have the red swollen tonsils that come with a sore throat your tonsils may not stand out. Here's how to get a good look at them.

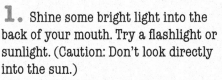

YOU NEED:
- a bright light source
- a tongue depressor (something flat like a clean popsicle stick works)
- a mirror (magnifying mirror is best)

1. Shine some bright light into the back of your mouth. Try a flashlight or sunlight. (Caution: Don't look directly into the sun.)

2. Press your tongue down and out of the way with a depressor.

3. See your uvula? It the little punching bag–shaped thing that hangs down from the roof of your mouth. Now look for the extra pink bits of flesh on either side of the uvula. Those are your palatine tonsils.

4. You can use a clean Q-tip to lift the tonsil flaps in the back of the throat to get a better look.

TONSILLITIS

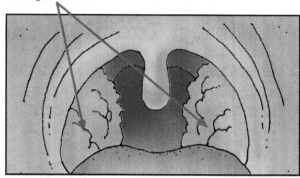

Enlarged tonsils

Sometimes a strain of bad microbes moves into your tonsils and throat and overwhelms your normal microbe community. The intruders disrupt the balance between your immune system and your resident microbes. Your body's defenses spring into action. Your throat feels swollen, hot and sore. Generally, the balance is restored and you return to health.

Sometimes the infection is stubborn and doesn't go away after a few days. A doctor might take a throat culture by rubbing a giant cotton swab on your tonsils, then send it to a lab to determine what critters are making you sick. Your doctor might prescribe antibiotics that will kill a good number of bad microbes (and some of your good microbes in the bargain). After the antibiotic does its work, the body's natural defenses knock off the rest of the problem bacteria.

CASE OF THE MISSING TONSILS

FACT: *Tonsillectomy is the name of an operation to remove tonsils.*

Not so long ago a lot of kids in America were missing their tonsils. In the 1950s, if there was a little bit of tonsil swelling, doctors would cut them out. They thought tonsils didn't do much. Now we know tonsils do an important job, so removing them is considered only as a last resort.

Troublemaking bacteria can sometimes fester and hide in your tonsils. Your throat can even get so inflamed and swollen with infection that you can't eat or breathe. Then a tonsillectomy can save your life.

Activity: Tonsil Survey

Tonsillectomy has been around for about 3,000 years and it goes in and out of style. Do you have your tonsils? Does your mom? How about your grandmother? Survey your family and friends to find out who has had their tonsils removed.

YOU NEED:
• pencil and paper

1. First record the age of the person.

2. Ask them if they still have their tonsils.

3. If not, ask when and why they were removed.

4. Do this for a number of people. Try and ask both young and older folks

Notice: Are more young or older people missing their tonsils? Do you find a pattern?

Tonsil Survey

1. Name / Age

2. Tonsils removed? / Yes or No?

3. If yes, what year?

4. Why?

ROCKS
IN YOUR MOUTH?

Did you know your tonsils can grow stones? Sometimes chalky deposits collect in the tonsils. Tonsil stones are knots of hardened biofilm containing living and dead bacteria, dead cells and mucus.

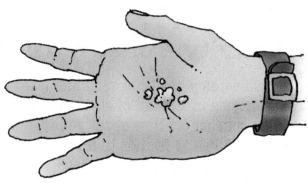

STINKY STUFF

Tonsil stones can be smelly. When some mouth bacteria break down food bits and dead cells, they make sulfur compounds. When this sulfur is released into the air, it stinks! Skunk, garlic, rotten eggs all owe their stinky smells to sulfur compounds. Stinky sulfur is added to odorless natural gas because it so attention getting.

Fusobacterium nucleatum:
aka: Nuc

DESCRIPTION

Nuc are rod- and spindle-shaped bacteria. They are excellent stickers.

HABITAT

Nuc are very common and are likely stuck to your teeth right now. They are an important part of your teeth biofilms. They can live either with or without much oxygen. Sometimes they enter the bloodstream through wounds and cause infections in other parts of the body, including the lungs, heart and skin.

LIFESTYLE

Nuc are not first in line to form biofilms, but they are friends with everybody. Microbiologists call them great aggregators because they stick to a wide range of microbes. Because they are so good at sticking microbes together, they are major players in forming plaque. Their diet includes many different proteins and carbohydrates. They are especially good at getting energy from different kinds of sugars.

SPECIAL TALENTS

Besides being extremely sticky, Nuc can hide inside surface cells where they can't be found by your defense cells. This makes Nuc difficult to study.

GIANT TONSIL STONES

If you had a gigantic tonsil stone you might notice a feeling of something stuck in your throat. Other symptoms include difficulty swallowing, a metallic taste in the mouth, coughing fits, earache, swollen tonsils and bad breath. Generally, tonsil stones look like whitish or yellowish spots hanging on your tonsils at the back of the throat. It's easy to check: Just open wide and shine a light on the back of your mouth.

Look for tonsil stones here.

PROBING THE STONES

FACT: *Tonsillolith is another name for tonsil stone.*

A team of Japanese scientists extracted tonsil stones from six people with good oral hygiene habits but bad breath. They crushed the stones (yes, they do stink) and analyzed the DNA to find out what microbes were present. Researchers found a large diversity of stink-making bacteria. No two subjects had the same microbe mix, but all carried a least one type of odor-producing bacteria. These types of bacteria produce chemicals with a reputation for being highly smelly.

Chapter 8

BUDDIES FOR LIFE

Your Magnificent Microbes

Most of us humans think of microbes as mean, nasty, invisible disease-causing germs that deserve a quick death.

Microbes deserve your respect. The truth is that microbes are major players in life on Earth. They do important jobs like recycling nutrients back into the soil. They purify our water. They put the bubbles in beer, the tang in yogurt and make bread rise. Without microbes, life as we know it would come to a grinding halt.

Microbes are the invisible majority on Earth. Not only do they live in soil, water and air, they live on you and in you, occupying your every nook and cranny. The idea that we can rid ourselves of microbes is, well, ridiculous. Besides, why would you want

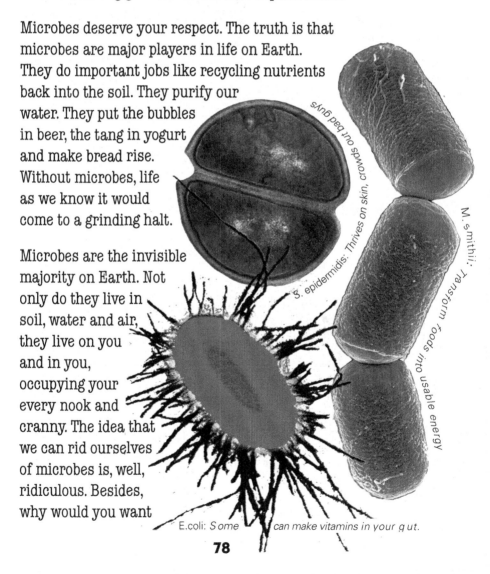

S. epidermidis: Thrives on skin, crowds out bad guys

M. smithii: Transform foods into usable energy

E.coli: Some _____ can make vitamins in your gut.

to? Most microbes do you no harm. True, a few can cause disease, but generally your body's defenses easily fend them off.

Some microbes even do you some big favors. We know that they help digest your food. They make vitamin K, which helps your blood clot. They help manufacture oils that keep your skin soft. We are just beginning to understand some of the many ways microbes keep us healthy.

BEYOND SICK
THE HUMAN MICROBIOME PROJECT

The National Institutes of Health decided to find out exactly how many microbes called healthy people home. In 2007 they launched a giant study called the Human Microbiome Project. They began by sampling microbes from about 15 different body sites on about 300 healthy volunteers. Over a period of 2 years, they collected more than 11,000 samples.

Two hundred scientists from around the world began sorting the samples with new DNA identification tools. They were able to identify the DNA present in the samples. With this information, the scientists could recognize the many different types of microbe cells present on humans. The project cost millions of dollars and the work continues.

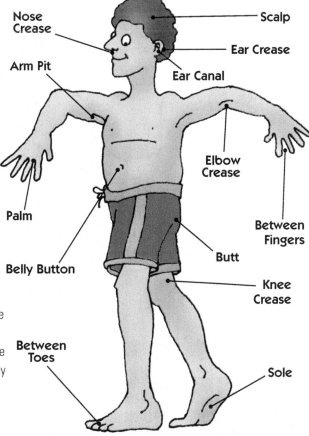

Very different bacteria colonize different sites on the body.

SCIENTISTS DISCOVER SOME
AMAZING THINGS

Normal healthy humans are home to trillions of microbes. There are thousands of different types or species that can live on and in us. For every human cell in your body there is at least one microbe cell. (Some estimates say more.) Because microbes are small they make up only about 2% of our body weight.

If you count the genes present in our bodies, our human cells contain about 20,000 genes and the microbes in our bodies give us 8,000,000 more genes.

BEST GUESS

No one knows for sure how many microbes live on a human. The best scientists can do is to give you an estimate. But the estimate changes as new information is discovered. New discoveries are being made all the time.

GENE SUPER POWERS

Think of genes as instruction packets packed in our cells. All these extra genes give us superpowers. For instance, our gut bacteria have instructions for breaking down foods that we could not digest on our own. The bacteria are able to convert a common food preservative called benzoate into a useful compound that our bodies need in order to make biotin, one of the B vitamins. Others help strengthen our intestinal walls — helping to keep us healthy by making it harder for dangerous compounds

GOOD GERMS

Healthy people carry disease-causing microbes. This is normal. Having microbes doesn't make you sick.

In fact, the opposite seems to be true: Having germs in many ways makes you healthy. It's only now that we are learning how.

New research has given us some answers, but with new discoveries come more questions. That's how science works. As we learn more, we also learn more about what we don't know. With microbes there is still a lot to discover. But one thing we know for sure: Germs are not all bad. Often, microbes are good to have on your team.

YOU'RE SPECIAL

Everyone carries a unique mix of microbes. We each have a signature set: Some are common, some rare. There are big differences among people. You have some bacteria in common with the person sitting next to you, but you also have many that are just your own. The bacteria inside us can vary as much as 80% from one person to another. Microbes "pinch hit" for each other. Our body has certain jobs that need doing, like digesting fat. The microbes that digest your friend's fat are not necessarily the same kind that digest fat for you.

SO WATCH YOUR MOUTH! *You just might discover something new!*

And don't forget to floss!

ACKNOWLEDGEMENTS

Watch Your Mouth! is one of several products of the Biology of Human project, funded by the National Institutes of Health (NIH) through the Science Education Partnership Award (SEPA) Grant No. R25OD010506. Its content is solely the responsibility of the authors and does not necessarily represent the official views of the NIH. Principal investigators are Judy Diamond, University of Nebraska State Museum; Julia McQuillan, Department of Sociology at the University of Nebraska – Lincoln; and Charles Wood, Nebraska Center for Virology. This book is a collaboration with the Science & Health Education Partnership at UC San Francisco (http://ucsf.edu/sep).

Many scientists and educators guided our work and reviewed its production. Foremost, we acknowledge the assistance of Gary Armitage, D.D.S., Professor, School of Dentistry at UC San Francisco, who graciously reviewed all of the book's content. We also thank Amy Spiegel Ph.D., Patricia Wonch Hill Ph.D., Abby Heithoff, Ilonka Zlatar, Sara LeRoy Toren, Adam Wagler, Daniel Cassel, Kai Cassel, and the staff of the University of Nebraska Bureau of Sociological Research. Students at Culler Middle School (Lincoln, Nebraska) assisted in testing the activities in this book. We are grateful to co-investigators Charles Wood and Julia McQuillan for their inspiration and guidance. Thanks to Susan Foster, Tracy Tandy, and Stella Allison for their editing assistance. We also thank George Little D.D.S. of Ross Family Dentistry (Ross, California) and the students at UCSF School of Dentistry for sharing their ideas about teaching oral health. Finally, this book would not have been possible without the encouragement and support of our NIH-SEPA program officer, Tony Beck.

For more information about our projects visit: **http://biologyofhuman.unl.edu**

ABOUT THE AUTHORS

Linda Allison is an author and illustrator of more than a dozen books, including the *New York Times* bestseller *Blood and Guts: A Working Guide to Your Own Insides*. She has created digital learning tools and museum educational projects, and she is a literacy coach. A graduate of the University of California Berkeley College of Environmental Design, Linda has applied her natural curiosity to a wide variety of topics, from the human body to fabric inventions to the wildlife within the home. She is fascinated by adventure travel, visual humor and any kind of creative mischief.

Rebecca Smith is a scientist-educator who has supported science teaching and learning in the San Francisco public schools for more than 20 years. As Co-Director of the UC San Francisco Science & Health Education Partnership, Rebecca has designed innovative learning experiences that engage students, from youths to adults, as scientists in the classroom, helping them to discover big ideas in science, learn how to think critically, and make conclusions using evidence. Rebecca is a contributing author of *STEM to Story: Enthralling and Effective Lesson Plans for Grades 5–8* and the webcomic *Occupied*. When not sharing her passion for science, Rebecca can be found relaxing with her children, baking or making chocolate.

Judy Diamond is professor and curator of informal science education at the University of Nebraska State Museum. A biologist and science educator, she is the author of over 40 publications on informal learning. Her long career working in science museums began at the Lawrence Hall of Science at UC Berkeley and the Exploratorium in San Francisco. She is lead author of *Kea, Bird of Paradox: The Evolution and Behavior of a New Zealand Parrot* (University of California Press, 1999), editor, *Virus and the Whale: Exploring Evolution in Creatures Small and Large* (National Science Teachers Association Press, 2006), and co-author, *Concealing Coloration in Animals* (Belknap/Harvard University Press, 2013).

William Wells is a designer and illustrator with over 40 years experience designing educational projects ranging from permanent museum exhibitions to interpretive products and graphics. He has a bachelor of science from the University of Oregon and a bachelor of fine arts from Art Center College of Design and has designed and illustrated over 30 books and other learning materials.

PHOTO CREDITS

PAGE 3 - *Streptococcus mutans*. Rod and coccoid bacteria from the human tongue. Photographer: Dr. Dennis Kunkel / Visuals Unlimited, Inc.

PAGE 5 - Human tooth enamel (yellow) with bacteria (blue) and red blood cells (red). Photographer: Thierry Berrod / Visuals Unlimited, Inc.

PAGE 6 - Pseudomonas bacterium with flagella. Photographer: Dr. Dennis Kunkel / Visuals Unlimited, Inc.

PAGE 7 - Chain of streptococcus bacteria. Photographer: Dr. David Phillips / Visuals Unlimited, Inc.

PAGE 10 - Dental plaque and oral microorganisms. SEM X4400. Photographer: Dr. Stanley Flegler / Visuals Unlimited, Inc.

PAGE 12 - *Streptococcus mutans* and *Bacteroides gingivalis*, and yeast (*Candida albicans*). SEM X2000. Photographer: Dr. Dennis Kunkel / Visuals Unlimited, Inc.

PAGE 13 - Human tooth enamel surface. SEM X435. Photographer: Dr. Dennis Kunkel / Visuals Unlimited, Inc.

PAGE 13 - Dental X-ray showing caries or tooth decay, popularly called cavities. Photographer: Dr. John D. Cunningham / Visuals Unlimited, Inc.

PAGE 15 - Human tooth fractured enamel. X400. Photographer: Dr. Dennis Kunkel / Visuals Unlimited, Inc.

PAGE 15 - Human tooth section showing enamel rods. SEM X1166. Photographer: Fred Hossler / Visuals Unlimited, Inc.

PAGE 16 - *Streptococcus mutans*. Rod and coccoid bacteria from the human tongue. Photographer: Dr. Dennis Kunkel / Visuals Unlimited, Inc.

PAGE 18 - Chicken egg shell, fractured. SEM X18. Photographer: Dr. Wolf Fahrenbach / Visuals Unlimited, Inc.

PAGE 18 - Human tooth fractured enamel. SEM X400. Dr. Dennis Kunkel / Visuals Unlimited, Inc.

PAGE 22 - Fluorite, from Chengdu, China. Photographer: Dane Johnson / Visuals Unlimited, Inc.

PAGE 22 - Human tooth enamel surface. SEM X435. Photographer: Dr. Dennis Kunkel / Visuals Unlimited, Inc.

PAGE 24 - Human skull. Photographer: Jarrod Erbe / Visuals Unlimited, Inc.

PAGE 25 - Biofilm on a stainless steel surface. SEM X1600. Photographer: Dr. Dennis Kunkel / Visuals Unlimited, Inc.

PAGE 25 - Dental plaque. Photographer: Dr. Gary Gaugler/ Visuals Unlimited, Inc.

PAGE 32 - Used wax dental floss with dental plaque (green), bacteria (orange) and cheek cells (red) on the dental floss fibers (blue). SEM X70. Photographer: Dr. Dennis Kunkel / Visuals Unlimited, Inc.

PAGE 33 - Inner surface of a medical catheter infected with the yeast (*Candida albicans*), which can result in serious tissue infections. Photographer: Dr. Dennis Kunkel / Visuals Unlimited, Inc.

PAGE 35 - DNA (fingerprint) separation on agarose gel. Photographer: Jarrod Erbe / Visuals Unlimited, Inc.

PAGE 35 - *Streptococcus mutans* bacteria on the human tongue. Photographer: Dr. Dennis Kunkel / Visuals Unlimited, Inc.

PAGE 36 - *Streptococcus mutans* bacteria. TEM X27000. Photographer: Science VU / Visuals Unlimited, Inc.

PAGE 46 - Mammal tongue papillae and taste bud. SEM X52. Photographer: Dr. Dennis Kunkel / Visuals Unlimited, Inc.

PAGE 47 - *Treponema denticola*. TEM X2100. Photographer: Dr. Terry Beveridge / Visuals Unlimited, Inc.

PAGE 54 - Cells in potato with starch stained purple. LM X83. Photographer: George Wilder / Visuals Unlimited, Inc.

PAGE 56 - Bacteriophage viruses escaping from a dying streptococcus bacteria cell. SEM X21335. Photographer: Dr. Dennis Kunkel / Visuals Unlimited, Inc.

PAGE 59 - Bacterial shapes, rod, cocci, and spiral from the mouth. SEM X5000. Photographer: doc-stock / Visuals Unlimited, Inc.

PAGE 61 - Yeast (*Candida albicans*) on the filiform papillae of the tongue. SEM X600. Photographer: Dr. Stanley Flegler / Visuals Unlimited, Inc.

PAGE 62 - Mammal tongue papillae and taste bud. SEM X52. Photographer: Dr. Dennis Kunkel / Visuals Unlimited, Inc.

PAGE 64 - *Streptococcus mutans* bacteria on the human tongue. Photographer: Dr. Dennis Kunkel / Visuals Unlimited, Inc.

PAGE 64 - Tongue showing filiform papillae. SEM X165. Photographer: Dr. Richard Kessel & Dr. Randy Kardon/ Visuals Unlimited, Inc.

PAGE 67 - Bacillus bacteria forming a biofilm. SEM X2200. Photographer: Dr. Dennis Kunkel / Visuals Unlimited, Inc.

PAGE 68 - The yeast *Candida albicans*. Photographer: Dr. Dennis Kunkel / Visuals Unlimited, Inc.

PAGE 69 - Mixed oral bacteria. Photographer: David Phillips / Visuals Unlimited, Inc.

PAGE 70 - Human tonsils removed during an operation. Photographer: Ralph Hutchings / Visuals Unlimited, Inc.

PAGE 71 - Pus in human inflamed tonsils consisting of a variety of bacteria. Photographer: Simko / Visuals Unlimited, Inc.

PAGE 71 - Palatine tonsil section. LM X3. Photographer: Dr. John D. Cunningham / Visuals Unlimited, Inc.

PAGE 76 - *Fusobacterium nucleatum*. SEM X3250. Photographer: Dr. Dennis Kunkel / Visuals Unlimited, Inc.

PAGE 78 - *Staphylococcus epidermidis* is a part of the normal flora in the intestines, skin and upper respiratory tract. TEM X104400. Photographer: George Musil / Visuals Unlimited, Inc.

PAGE 78 - *Methanobrevibacter smithii* bacteria. SEM. Photographer: Dr. Dennis Kunkel / Visuals Unlimited, Inc.

PAGE 78 - *Escherichia coli* is a rod shaped bacteria that can cause urinary tract infections, traveler's diarrhea. TEM X5000. Photographer: Dr. Dennis Kunkel / Visuals Unlimited, Inc.

LEGEND

LM = Light Microscope

SEM = Scanning Electron Microscope

TEM = Transmission Electron Microscope

CPSIA information can be obtained
at www.ICGtesting.com
Printed in the USA
LVOW06s0856020816
497978LV00004B/5/P